DIRECTORY OF SOCIAL WELFARE RESEARCH CAPABILITIES

A Working Guide to Organizations Engaged in Social Work and Social Welfare Research

RICHARD J. ESTES

Director,
Center for the Study of Social Work Practice
University of Pennsylvania

Research Report No. 80-12

DORRANCE & COMPANY • *Ardmore, Pennsylvania*

Acknowledgments

The research reported in this volume was made possible, in part, through support from the Esther Lazarus-Albert D. Goldman endowment to the Center for the Study of Social Work Practice and from the general research funds of the School of Social Work of the University of Pennsylvania. Research assistance was provided by James Power. James Carpenter, Ivo Reznicek and Ruall Jordan-Cook provided valuable consultation to the author during the early stages of the survey. Joan Habres typed the several versions of the manuscript and Deborah Masi provided critically needed administrative support. These persons are thanked for their good spirits, cooperation, and contribution to the DIRECTORY'S completion.

The directors and coordinators of social welfare research centers throughout the United States are acknowledged and thanked for their cooperation with the various phases of this project. Dean Louise Shoemaker is gratefully acknowledged for her continuing support of the research activities of the Center.

Library of Congress Catalog Card No. 80–70895
ISBN 0–8059–2788–3
Manufactured in the United States of America

TO: Lynn, Vicki, Jennifer

Contents

The CENTER FOR THE STUDY OF SOCIAL WORK
PRACTICE is an intergral part of the research and
educational programs of the University of Pennsylvania School of Social Work. The activities of the Center
are both national and local in scope and are organized
around the achievement of one objective: systematic
inquiry into the theory and knowledge base underlying
professional social work as practiced in a variety of
forms across a broad range of institutional settings.

Introduction

The publication of this expanded DIRECTORY OF SOCIAL WELFARE RESEARCH CAPABILITIES is a tribute to the increasing capacity of social welfare agencies and organizations for engaging in systematic study of their activities. The DIRECTORY is a tribute, too, to the hundreds of men and women who long have sought to make research an integral part of the social work practice field.

The DIRECTORY lists seventy-five (75) social welfare related research units located in twenty-five states and the Commonwealth of Puerto Rico. These research units were identified as part of a nationwide survey focused on assessing the research capabilities of social work and social work related organizations. In all, some 200 social work organizations and agencies were surveyed during Spring, 1980. Of the 75 Centers listed in the DIRECTORY forty-four (44) are located within university settings—of which forty-one (41) are affiliated with graduate schools of social work—fifteen (15) are departments within large national social welfare service agencies, and sixteen (16) are units within national social welfare professional associations or organizations.

The DIRECTORY provides the user with detailed information for individual Centers in relation to Center *auspice, relationship to sponsoring institution* or *organization, organizing research purpose(s), major research interests* and *activities, size* and *composition of research staff, funding patterns,* and *research publications information.* Information also is provided to enable users to contact Centers directly for details regarding other aspects of Center activities not described in the DIRECTORY. Consumers and financial supporters of social welfare research should find the DIRECTORY to be of help in identifying those Centers engaged in research of particular interest to the user. Teachers of research, social agency personnel, research center staff, social work students, and others should also find the DIRECTORY to be of value in requesting specialized information and technical assistance from individual Centers.

Richard J. Estes, DSW
Center for Study of Social Work
Practice
University of Pennsylvania
November, 1980

1

How To Use the Directory

The DIRECTORY is divided into five (5) sections:

I. *Alphabetical Listing of Social Welfare Research Centers by Name, Auspice, State and Code Numbers*

II. *Listing of Social Welfare Research Centers by Code Number, Name, Auspice and State*

III. *Alphabetical Listing of Research Center Contact persons by Title and Center Number*

IV. *Individual Research Centers by State and Directory Code Numbers*

V. *Center Research Priorities by Substantive Area and Center Code Number*

Center Code Numbers

Each Center indexed into the DIRECTORY has been assigned a six-digit code, e.g., the *Center for the Study of Social Work Practice* is coded as "215011." Center codes have been assigned as follows:

Digits 1–3 (e.g. "215"): Telephone Area Code within which the Center is located.

Digits 4–5 (e.g. "01"): Directory entry order of the Center by State within which Center is located.

Digit 6 (e.g. "1"): Center's Principal Auspice
1 = School of Social Work Auspice
2 = University Auspice
3 = National Voluntary Organization Auspice
4 = Municipal Government Auspice
5 = State Government Auspice
6 = Federal Government Auspice
7 = International Organization Auspice

Future entries into the DIRECTORY will be assigned Center code numbers consistent with the preceding classification scheme.

Research Priority Code Numbers

The research priorities of individual centers are grouped in four cate-

gories: 1) *Social Work Profession Focussed*; 2) *Social Work Fields of Practice*; 3) *Special Populations*; and, 4) *Social Work Practice Modes*.
The following codes are used to identify priorities for each category:

1. *Profession Focussed*

History	1
Manpower	2
Education/Training	3
Ethics/Values	4
Interprofessional Relationships	5
Professional Community Relations	6
Standards/Practices	7
Service Utilization	8
Service Effectiveness	9
Benefit/Cost Analysis	10

2. *Fields of Practice*

Aging/Aged	11
Alcoholism/Drug Addiction	12
Crime/Delinquency	13
Economic Security	14
Family/Child Welfare	15
Health/Medical Care	16
Mental Health	17
Mental Retardation	18
Physically Handicapped	19
Housing/Urban Development	20
Early Childhood Education	21
Civil Rights/Civil Liberties	22
Employment/Unemployment	23
Other Fields of Practice	(as specified)

3. *Special Populations*

Poor	24
Minorities	25
Women	26
Youth	27
Other Populations	(as speci- fied)

4. *Practice Modes*

Social Casework	30
Social Group Work	31
Community Organ- ization	32
Social Administration	33
Social Planning	34
Social Policy Analysis	35
Social Work Research	36
Consultation	37
Social Work Education	38

Updating and/or Correcting DIRECTORY Information

From time to time Center Directors will want to update or correct DIRECTORY information describing individual Center activities. To effect these changes, Directors should photocopy the most recent DIRECTORY entry for their Center and hand write the changes which are to be made on the photocopied entry. The revised entry should be signed by the Director and forwarded directly to the author at the following address: Center for the Study of Social Work Practice, University of Pennsylvania, School of Social Work, 3701 Locust Walk, Philadelphia, Pennsylvania 19104. Centers not presently listed in the DIRECTORY may have their organizations included in future editions of this publication by completing the summary questionnaire reprinted in Appendix A. The completed questionnaire should be returned as indicated above.

I ALPHABETICAL LISTING OF SOCIAL WELFARE
RESEARCH CENTERS BY NAME, AUSPICE, STATE
AND CODE NUMBER

Adelphi University, (New York) 516011

American Correctional Association, (Maryland) 301023

American Foundation for the Blind, (New York) 212133

American Home Economics Association, (District of Columbia) 202063

American Planning Association, (District of Columbia) 202073

American Public Health Association, (District of Columbia) 202093

American Public Welfare Association, (District of Columbia) 202043

Association for Retarded Citizens, (Texas) 817033

Center for Advanced Studies in Human Services, University of Wisconsin at Milwaukee, (Wisconsin) 414011

Center for Employment and Income Studies, Brandeis University (Massachusetts) 617031

Center for Evaluation Research, Training and Program Development, University of Wisconsin at Madison, (Wisconsin) 608021

Center for Health Policy Analysis and Research, Brandeis University (Massachusetts) 617051

Center for Evaluation Research, Training and Program Development, University of Wisconsin at Madison, (Wisconsin) 608021

Center for International and Comparative Social Welfare, Rutgers University, (New Jersey) 201022

Center for Research, Evaluation, Training, University of Minnesota, (Minnesota) 218011

Center for Social Policy and Community Development, Temple University (Pennsylvania) 215021

Center for Social Research and Development, University of Denver (Colorado) 303012

Center for Social Services Evaluation and Research, University of Houston (Texas) 713011

Center for Social Welfare Research, University of Washington (Washington) 206011

Center for Social Work Research, University of Texas at Austin (Texas) 512031

Center for the Study of Social Welfare Policy, University of Chicago (Illinois) 202131

Center for the Study of Social Work Practice, University of Pennsylvania (Pennsylvania) 215011

Congress on Racial Equality, (New York) 212093

Council on Social Work Education, (New York) 212113

9

Data Center, Young Women's Christian Association (New York) 212023

Florence G. Heller—JWB Research Center, (New York) 212033

Foster Parents Plan International, (Rhode Island) 401013

Girl Scouts of the U.S.A., (New York) 212123

Human Services Design Laboratory, Case Western Reserve University (Ohio) 216011

Institute for Socioeconomic Studies, (New York) 914013

Jane Addams Center for Social Policy and Research, University of Illinois at Chicago Circle (Illinois) 312011

John F. Kennedy Center for Research on Education and Human Development, (Tennessee) 615012

Levinson Policy Institute, Brandeis University (Massachusetts) 617021

National Aging Policy Center in Income Maintenance, Brandeis University (Massachusetts) 617041

National Association for the Advancement of Colored People, (New York) 212043

National Association of Housing and Redevelopment Officials, (District of Columbia) 202013

National Association of Social Workers, (District of Columbia) 202083

National Child Labor Committee, (New York) 212063

National Committee Against Discrimination in Housing, (District of Columbia) 202103

National Conference on Social Welfare, (District of Columbia) 202023

National Council for Homemakers—Home Health Aide Services, Inc., (New York) 212083

National Easter Seals Society, Inc., (Illinois) 312043

National Housing Conference, (District of Columbia) 202113

National Urban Coalition, (District of Columbia) 202033

Parents Without Partners, (District of Columbia) 301033

Regional Research Institute for Human Services, Portland State University (Oregon) 503011

Research and Demonstration Center, Atlanta University (Georgia) 404011

Research Center, Adelphi University (New York) 212141

Research Center, Child Welfare League of America (New York) 212103

Research Center, Fordham University at Lincoln Center (New York) 212011

Research Center, Smith College (Massachusetts) 413011

Research Center, University of Connecticut (Connecticut) 203011

Research Center, University of Maryland (Maryland) 301011

Research Center, University of Texas at Arlington (Texas) 817021

Research Committee, West Virginia University (West Virginia) 304011

Research Department, Family Service Association of America (New York) 212073

Research Department, Public Administration Service (Illinois) 312033

Research Institute, University of Georgia (Georgia) 404021

Research Unit, University of Kentucky (Kentucky) 502011

Research and Demonstration Center, Columbia University (New York) 212151

School of Social Work, Boston University (Massachusetts) 617011

School of Social Work, University of Iowa (Iowa) 319011

Scientific Research Institute, University of Puerto Rico (Puerto Rico) 809011

Social Welfare Development and Research Center, University of Hawaii (Hawaii) 808011

Social Work Research Center, California State University Sacramento (California) 916011

Social Work Research Center, Howard University (District of Columbia) 202121

Social Work Research Center, Louisiana State University (Louisiana) 504021

Social Work Research Center, Loyola University of Chicago (Chicago) 312021

Social Work Research Center, Rutgers University (New Jersey) 201011

Social Work Research Center, Tulane University (Louisiana) 504011

Social Work Research Institute, University of Southern Mississippi (Mississippi) 601011

Society for Hospital Social Work Directors, (Illinois) 312053

United Neighborhood Centers of America, (New York) 212053

Urban Center, San Francisco State University (California) 415011

Veterans Administration, (District of Columbia) 202056

Western Regional Institute for the Study of Rural Human Services, California State University, Fresno (California) 209011

II LISTING OF SOCIAL WELFARE RESEARCH
    CENTERS BY CODE NUMBER, NAME, AUSPICE,
    AND STATE

Code	Name and University Auspice (State)
201011	*Social Work Research Center*, Rutgers University (New Jersey)
201022	*Center for International and Comparative Social Welfare*, Rutgers University (New Jersey)
202013	*National Association of Housing and Redevelopment Officials*, (District of Columbia)
202023	*National Conference on Social Welfare*, (District of Columbia)
202033	*The National Urban Coalition*, (District of Columbia)
202043	*American Public Welfare Association*, (District of Columbia)
202056	*Veterans Administration*, (District of Columbia)
202063	*American Home Economics Association*, (District of Columbia)
202073	*American Planning Association*, (District of Columbia)
202083	*National Association of Social Workers*, (District of Columbia)
202093	*American Public Health Association*, (District of Columbia)
202103	*National Committee Against Discrimination in Housing*, (District of Columbia)
202113	*National Housing Conference*, (District of Columbia)
202121	*Social Work Research Center*, Howard University (District of Columbia)
202131	*Center for the Study of Social Welfare Policy*, University of Chicago (Illinois)
203011	*Research Center*, University of Connecticut (Connecticut)
206011	*Center for Social Welfare Research*, University of Washington (Washington)
209011	*Western Regional Institute for the Study of Rural Human Services*, California State University, Fresno (California)
212011	*Research Center,* Fordham University at Lincoln Center (New York)
212023	*Data Center*, Young Women's Christian Association (New York)
212033	*Florence G. Heller—JWB Research Center*, (New York)
212043	*National Association for the Advancement of Colored People*, (New York)

212053	*United Neighborhood Centers of America*, (New York)
212063	*National Child Labor Committee*, (New York)
212073	*Research Department*, Family Service Association of America (New York)
212083	*National Council for Homemakers—Home Health Aide Services, Inc.*, (New York)
212093	*Congress on Racial Equality*, (New York)
212103	*Research Center*, Child Welfare League of America (New York)
212113	*Council on Social Work Education*, (New York)
212123	*Girl Scouts of the U.S.A.*, (New York)
212133	*American Foundation for the Blind*, (New York)
212141	*Research Center*, Adelphi University (New York)
212151	*Research and Demonstration Center*, Columbia University (New York)
215011	*Center for the Study of Social Work Practice*, University of Pennsylvania (Pennsylvania)
215021	*Center for Social Policy and Community Development*, Temple University (Pennsylvania)
216011	*Human Services Design Laboratory*, Case Western Reserve University (Ohio)
218011	*Center for Research, Evaluation, Training*, University of Minnesota (Minnesota)
301011	*Research Center*, University of Maryland (Maryland)
301023	*American Correctional Association*, (Maryland)
301033	*Parents Without Partners*, (District of Columbia)
303012	*Center for Social Research and Development*, University of Denver (Colorado)
304011	*Research Committee*, West Virginia University (West Virginia)
312011	*Jane Addams Center for Social Policy and Research*, University of Illinois at Chicago Circle (Illinois)
312021	*Social Work Research Center*, Loyola University of Chicago (Illinois)
312033	*Research Department*, Public Administration Service (Illinois)
312043	*National Easter Seals Society, Inc.*, (Illinois)

312053	*Society for Hospital Social Work Directors*, (Illinois)
319011	*School of Social Work*, University of Iowa (Iowa)
401013	*Foster Parents Plan International*, (Rhode Island)
404011	*Research and Demonstration Center*, Atlanta University (Georgia)
404021	*Research Institute*, University of Georgia (Georgia)
413011	*Research Center*, Smith College (Massachusetts)
414011	*Center for Advanced Studies in Human Services*, University of Wisconsin at Milwaukee (Wisconsin)
415011	*Urban Center*, San Francisco State University (California)
502011	*Research Unit*, University of Kentucky (Kentucky)
503011	*Regional Research Institute for Human Services*, Portland State University (Oregon)
504011	*Social Work Research Center*, Tulane University (Louisiana)
504021	*Social Work Research Center*, Louisiana State University (Louisiana)
512031	*Center for Social Work Research*, University of Texas at Austin (Texas)
516011	*Adelphi University* (New York)
601011	*Social Work Research Institute*, University of Southern Mississippi (Mississippi)
608021	*Center for Evaluation Research, Training and Program Development*, University of Wisonsin at Madison (Wisconsin)
615012	*John F. Kennedy Center for Research on Education and Human Development*, (Tennessee)
617011	*School of Social Work*, Boston University (Massachusetts)
617021	*Levinson Policy Institute*, Brandeis University (Massachusetts)
617031	*Center for Employment and Income Studies*, Brandeis University (Massachusetts)
617041	*National Aging Policy Center on Income Maintenance*, Brandeis University (Massachusetts)
617051	*Center for Health Policy Analysis and Research*, Brandeis University (Massachusetts)
713011	*Center for Social Services Evaluation and Research*, University of Houston (Texas)

808011	*Social Welfare Development and Research Center*, University of Hawaii (Hawaii)
809011	*Scientific Research Institute*, University of Puerto Rico (Puerto Rico)
817021	*Research Center*, University of Texas at Arlington (Texas)
817033	*Association for Retarded Citizens* (Texas)
914013	*The Institute for Socioeconomic Studies* (New York)
916011	*Social Work Research Center*, California State University Sacramento (California)

III ALPHABETICAL LISTING OF RESEARCH CENTER CONTACT PERSONS BY TITLE AND CENTER NUMBER

Adair, Alvis (Director) 202121

Almond, Inez L. (Director of Public Relations) 212053

Altman, Morton (Director) 212033

Austin, David M. (Administrator) 512031

Austin, Michael J. (Director) 206011

Baumheier, Edward C. (Director) 303012

Beck, Dorothy Fahs (Director) 212073

Betsy, Charles L. (Executive Director) 202033

Binstock, Robert (Director) 617041

Boehm, Werner W. (Director) 201022

Bowker, Lee H. (Director) 414011

Buttrick, Shirley (Director) 312011

Callahan, James (Director) 617021

Campbell, Margaret (Director) 504011

Carter, Irl (Dean) 218011

Craft, John (Director) 319011

Delbecq, Andre (Director) 608021

DiBella, Anthony J. (Assistant Director) 401013

Dodson, Jualynne (Director) 404011

Dolgoff, Ralph (Assistant Dean) 516011

Emlen, Arthur C. (Director) 503011

Erber, Ernest (Director) 202103

Estes, Richard J. (Director) 215011

Fanshell, David (Director) 212151

Farrow, Frank (Deputy Director) 202131/312061

Geismar, Ludwig L. (Director) 201011

Gellman, William (Director) 312043

Gochman, David S. (Director) 502011

Grenier, Charles (Research Chair) 504021

Hansan, John E. (Executive Director) 202023

Hausman, Leonard (Director) 617031

Heilman, Robert (Chair, Research Committee) 916011

Holmes, George (Communications Coordinator) 212093

Isralowitz, Richard E. (Director) 216011

Jennings, Daniel (Dean) 713011

Jones, Mary Ann (Director) 212103

Katz, Arthur (Executive Director) 212113

Kaye, Barbara (Accounts Manager) 202113

Kirchner, Corinne (Director) 212133

Levine, Alice (Executive) 212023

Linn, Margaret W. (Director) 202056

Lobb, Michael (Director) 817021

Lohmann, Roger A. (Coordinator) 304011

McBeath, William H. (Executive Director) 202093

Meyers, Michael (Assistant Director) 212043

Mosena, David R. (Director) 202073

Nagoshi, Jack T. (Director) 808011

Nenno, Mary K. (Associate Director) 202013

Neman, Ronald (Associate Director) 817033

Parks, Ann (Information Officer) 301033

Pinner, Elizabeth L. (Acting Director) 203011

Reilly, Charles (Dean) 312021

Richman, Harold (Director) 312061/202131

Rittersporn, B.A. (Program Director) 914013

Robertson, Angelika (Research Associate) 413011

Rodriquez, Carmen F. Q. (Director) 809011

Rosemergy, Janet M. (Coordinator of Information Services) 615012

Rosenthal, Seymour (Director) 215021

Rossen, Salie (Executive Director) 312053

Selzer, D. (Director) 212123

Sherwood, Clarence (Chairman) 617011

Shinn, Eugene L. (Director) 212011/212083

Sloane, John (Associate Dean) 415011

Slovak, Jeffrey S. (Director) 312033

Stern, Leonard W. (Associate Executive Director) 202083

Talbert, Wynn (Director) 209011

Tatara, Toshio (Director) 202043

Turem, Jerry S. (Director) 301011

Vaughn, Gladys Gary (Administrator) 202063

Wallack, Stanley (Director) 617051
Weissman, Rae (Research Associate) 212063
Wodarski, John (Director) 404021
Worrall, Jay (Program Director) 301023
Zimmerman, Jerome (Director) 601011

IV LISTING OF INDIVIDUAL RESEARCH CENTERS BY STATE AND DIRECTORY CODE NUMBERS

CODE NUMBER: 209011

CENTER NAME/
  ADDRESS: WESTERN REGIONAL INSTITUTE FOR THE
            STUDY OF RURAL HUMAN SERVICES
            California State University, Fresno (1966)
            Fresno, California 93740
            (209) 487-1192

CONTACT PERSON: Dr. Wynn Talbert
            (209) 487-1192

ADMINISTRATIVE UNIT: Integral unit of the School of Social Work,
            University of California at Fresno, Center will
            become operational during academic year
            1980–81.

BUDGET FY 1979–80:   Not available

STAFFING: PROFESSIONAL STAFF
            Social Work:
            Other Social Science:

            STUDENTS IN TRAINING
            Social Work:
            Other Social Science:

RESEARCH PURPOSES/
  ACTIVITIES: When operational, the Institute will provide for
            the research needs of students and faculty at
            the school, the University, and surrounding
            San Joaquin Valley Community.

RESEARCH PRIORITIES: *Profession Focussed:*   5, 6, 8, 9
            Fields of Practice: 16, 17, 21, Industrial
                        Social Services

            Special Populations:
            Practice Modes:

PUBLICATIONS: 1. Publications list available on request.

DATE RESEARCH UNIT
  ESTABLISHED: 1980

DIRECTORY ENTRY DATE: April, 1980

CODE NUMBER:	415011
CENTER NAME/ ADDRESS:	URBAN CENTER San Francisco State University 1600 Holloway Avenue San Francisco, California 94132 (415) 469-1005
CONTACT PERSON:	John Sloane, Associate Dean School of Behavioral and Social Sciences (415) 469-2409
ADMINISTRATIVE UNIT:	Center will be integral unit of the School of Behavioral and Social Sciences but will be administered by the Director of the Department of Social Work Education.
BUDGET FY 1979–80:	Not available
STAFFING:	*PROFESSIONAL STAFF* *Social Work:* *Other Social Science:* *STUDENTS IN TRAINING* *Social Work:* *Other Social Science:*
RESEARCH PURPOSES/ ACTIVITIES:	The Urban Center serves as an organizational framework for stimulating, developing, and evaluating research and research training activities at the School of Behavioral and Social Sciences at San Francisco State University.

RESEARCH PRIORITIES:

Profession Focussed:	3, 5, 6, 7, 8, 9
Fields of Practice:	All fields, Urban Social Work
Special Populations:	24, 25, 26, 27
Practice Modes:	All

PUBLICATIONS:	1. Publications list available on request.
DATA RESEARCH UNIT ESTABLISHED:	Will open February 1, 1981
DIRECTORY ENTRY DATE:	June, 1980

CODE NUMBER:	916011
CENTER NAME/	
ADDRESS:	SOCIAL WORK RESEARCH CENTER
	California State University, Sacramento (1966)
	6000 J. Street
	Sacramento, California 95819
	(916) 454-6121 or 7180
CONTACT PERSON:	Robert Heilman, Chair, Research Committee
ADMINISTRATIVE UNIT:	Will be integral unit of School of Social Work, California State University at Sacramento
BUDGET FY 1979–80:	Not yet operational
STAFFING:	*PROFESSIONAL STAFF*
	Social Work:
	Other Social Science:
	STUDENTS IN TRAINING
	Social Work:
	Other Social Science:
RESEARCH PURPOSES/	
ACTIVITIES:	To describe, analyze and study effects/impact of social work practice at community and state level in those areas of question where faculty and agencies share an interest and readiness for research.
RESEARCH PRIORITIES:	*Profession Focussed:*
	Fields of Practice:
	Special Populations:
	Practice Modes:
PUBLICATIONS:	1. Publications list available on request.
DATE RESEARCH UNIT	
ESTABLISHED:	Planned to open AY 1980–81
DIRECTORY ENTRY DATE:	June, 1980

CODE NUMBER:	303012
CENTER NAME/ ADDRESS:	CENTER FOR SOCIAL RESEARCH AND DEVELOPMENT University of Denver Denver, Colorado 80208 (303) 753-3464
CONTACT PERSON:	Edward C. Baumheier, Ph.D., Director (303) 753-3464
ADMINISTRATIVE UNIT:	Integral unit of Academic Research Center of the University of Denver
BUDGET FY 1979–80:	$350,000

STAFFING:

PROFESSIONAL STAFF

Social Work:	1 Full time
Other Social Science:	5 Full time; 2 Part time

STUDENTS IN TRAINING

Social Work:	1 M.S.W.
Other Social Science:	1 M.A.

RESEARCH PURPOSES/ ACTIVITIES:

The Center conducts applied social research focusing on social problems and policy issues relevant to local, regional, national and international concerns. Provides technical assistance and consulting services through its research utilization program to governmental agencies and non-profit community service organizations.

RESEARCH PRIORITIES:

Profession Focussed:	2, 3, 9
Fields of Practice:	11, 15, 16, 18, 19, 23
Special Populations:	24, 25 Native Americans
Practice Modes:	34, 35, 36, 37, 32

PUBLICATIONS:	1. Publications list available on request.
DATE RESEARCH UNIT ESTABLISHED:	1970
DIRECTORY ENTRY DATE:	June, 1980

CODE NUMBER: 203011
CENTER NAME/
  ADDRESS: RESEARCH CENTER
                          Graduate School of Social Work (1949)
                          University of Connecticut
                          Greater Hartford Campus
                          West Hartford, Connecticut 06117
                          (203) 523-4841

CONTACT PERSON: Dr. Elizabeth L. Pinner, Acting Director
                          (203) 523-4841

ADMINISTRATIVE UNIT: Integram unit of the Graduate School of
                          Social Work University of Connecticut, W.
                          Hartford.

BUDGET FY 1976–77:   Not available

STAFFING: *PROFESSIONAL STAFF*
                            Social Work: 1 Part time
                            Other Social Science: 1 Full time

                          STUDENTS IN TRAINING
                            Social Work: 2 Part time
                            Other Social Science: 0

RESEARCH PURPOSES/
  ACTIVITIES: To provide research services to interested
                          social agencies; and, technical assistance to
                          faculty in their own research activities.

RESEARCH PRIORITIES: *Profession Focussed:*   6
                          Fields of Practice: 16, School Social
                                                     Work
                          Special Populations:
                          Practice Modes: Social Work Practice,
                                                     33

PUBLICATIONS: 1. Publications list available on request.

DATE RESEARCH UNIT
  ESTABLISHED:

DIRECTORY ENTRY DATE: 1978

CODE NUMBER:	202013
CENTER NAME/	
ADDRESS:	NATIONAL ASSOCIATION OF HOUSING AND REDEVELOPMENT OFFICIALS (1933)
	2600 Virginia Avenue, N.W.
	Suite 404
	Washington, D.C. 20037
	(202) 333-2020
CONTACT PERSON:	Mary K. Nenno, Associate Director for Policy Development
	(202) 333-2020
ADMINISTRATIVE UNIT:	Research Development within the NAHRO
BUDGET FY 1979–80:	Not available

STAFFING:

PROFESSIONAL STAFF
  Social Work: Several full time

STUDENTS IN TRAINING
  Social Work:
  Other Social Science:

RESEARCH PURPOSES/   The Association collects and analyzes research data in the housing and community development field. Many special projects.

RESEARCH PRIORITIES:	*Profession Focussed:*	1, 2, 3, 4, 5, 6, 7, 8, 9, 10
	Fields of Practice:	20, Housing and Community Development
	Special Populations:	24
	Practice Modes:	34, 35

PUBLICATIONS: 1. Publications list available on request.

DATE RESEARCH UNIT
  ESTABLISHED:

DIRECTORY ENTRY DATE: June, 1980

CODE NUMBER: 202023

CENTER NAME/
  ADDRESS: NATIONAL CONFERENCE ON SOCIAL WEL-
                  FARE (1873)
                  1730 M Street, N.W.
                  Suite 911
                  Washington, D.C. 20036
                  (202) 785-0817

CONTACT PERSON: John E. Hansan, Ph.D., Executive Director

ADMINISTRATIVE UNIT: Research activities are an integral part of all
                  NCSW activities.

BUDGET FY 1979–80: $261,000

STAFFING: *PROFESSIONAL STAFF*
                  Social Work: 2 Full time
                  Other Social Science: 0
                  STUDENTS IN TRAINING
                  Social Work: 0
                  Other Social Science: 0

RESEARCH PURPOSES/
  ACTIVITIES: To provide a forum or conference as a means
                  of sharing information, serving as a clearing-
                  house and dissemination of research and
                  best practices in the field of social welfare.

RESEARCH PRIORITIES: *Profession Focussed:*   5, 6, 7, 8, 9
                  Fields of Practice: 18, Developmentally
                                          Disabled
                  Special Populations: Families
                  Practice Modes: 0

PUBLICATIONS: 1. *Social Welfare Forum* (Annual)

DATE RESEARCH UNIT
  ESTABLISHED: 1873

DIRECTORY ENTRY DATE: June, 1980

CODE NUMBER:	202033
CENTER NAME/	
ADDRESS:	URBAN POLICY, ANALYSIS AND RESEARCH UNIT The National Urban Coalition 1201 Connecticut Avenue N.W. Washington, D.C. 20036 (202) 331-2400
CONTACT PERSON:	Dr. Charles L. Betsey, Executive Director, Urban Policy Analysis and Research Unit (202) 331-2439
ADMINISTRATIVE UNIT:	The National Urban Coalition is an urban action, advocacy and information organization, bringing together business, labor, minorities, mayors and civic, community and religious backers to stabilize and revitalize American cities.
BUDGET FY 1979–80:	Budget not available

STAFFING:

PROFESSIONAL STAFF

Social Work:	0
Other Social Science:	4 Full time; 2 Part time

STUDENTS IN TRAINING

Social Work:	0
Other Social Science:	0

RESEARCH PURPOSES/
ACTIVITIES: The major purpose of the Urban Policy, Analysis and Research Unit is to increase the Coalition's in house capability to conduct analyses of Federal and State policies in urban areas and to increase the capacities of minorities and women in the policy process.

RESEARCH PRIORITIES:

Profession Focussed:	3,
Fields of Practice:	11, 14, 20, 22, 23, Urban Agenda for the 80's
Special Populations:	24, 25, 26, 27
Practice Modes:	32, 34, 45

PUBLICATIONS:	1. *Network* (Quarterly)
	2. *1980 Program and Budget* (Annual)
	3. *President's Report* (Annual)
	4. *Work and Training News* (Monthly)
	5. Many other special publications. Publications list available upon request.
DATE RESEARCH UNIT ESTABLISHED:	1918
DIRECTORY ENTRY DATE:	June, 1980

CODE NUMBER:	202043
CENTER NAME/ *ADDRESS:*	RESEARCH AND DEMONSTRATION DEPART-MENT American Public Welfare Association (1930) 1125 15th Street N.W., Suite 300 Washington, D.C. 20005 (202) 293-7550
CONTACT PERSON:	Toshio Tatara, Ph.D., Director, Research and Demonstration Department (202) 293-7550 Ext. 84
ADMINISTRATIVE UNIT:	Research is an integral part of all APWA activities
BUDGET FY 1979–80:	APWA = $1,000,000

STAFFING:

PROFESSIONAL STAFF

Social Work:	6 Full Time; 1 Part time
Other Social Science:	4 Full time; 2 Part time

STUDENTS IN TRAINING

Social Work:	0
Other Social Science:	0

RESEARCH PURPOSES/
ACTIVITIES:

To engage in research and demonstration activities which are supported by Federal and State human service agencies; to initiate research projects on topics which help member agencies with their information or knowledge needs; to provide member agencies with technical assistance related to capacity building in research.

RESEARCH PRIORITIES:

Profession Focussed:	2, 3, 6, 7, 8, 9
Fields of Practice:	14, 15, 16, 19, 22, Transportation
Special Populations:	24, 25, Indochinese Refugees
Practice Modes:	0

PUBLICATIONS: 1. *Public Welfare* (Quarterly)
                                      2. *The Welfare Memo* (Weekly)
                                      3. *Congressional Index* (Weekly)
                                      4. *Public Welfare Directory* (Yearly)
                                      5. *Washington Reports* (Monthly)

DATE RESEARCH UNIT
  ESTABLISHED: 1973
DIRECTORY ENTRY DATE: June, 1980

CODE NUMBER:	202056
CENTER NAME/	
ADDRESS:	VETERANS ADMINISTRATION (1930)
	810 Vermont Avenue, N.W.
	Washington, D.C. 20420
	(202) 389-2613
CONTACT PERSON:	Margaret W. Linn, Ph.D., Director of Social
	Science Research, V.A. Medical Center,
	Miami, FL 33125
	(305) 324-4455 Ext. 3585
ADMINISTRATIVE UNIT:	The Veterans Administration (V.A.) operates
	more than 150 Medical and Psychiatric facili-
	tes across the United States.
BUDGET FY 1979–80	$200,000

STAFFING:

PROFESSIONAL STAFF
- *Social Work:* 3 Full time
- *Other Social Science:* 3 Full time; 1 Part time

STUDENTS IN TRAINING
- *Social Work:* 0
- *Other Social Science:* 0

RESEARCH PURPOSES/ ACTIVITIES: The VA conducts psychosocial research which makes a knowledge contribution revelant to care of American veterans.

RESEARCH PRIORITIES:
- *Profession Focussed:* 9, 10
- *Fields of Practice:* 11, 12, 16, 17
- *Special Populations:* 24, 25, Veterans
- *Practice Modes* 0

PUBLICATIONS: 1. Publications list available on request.

DATE RESEARCH UNIT ESTABLISHED: 1965

DIRECTORY ENTRY DATE: June, 1980

CODE NUMBER:	202063
CENTER NAME/ ADDRESS:	AMERICAN HOME ECONOMICS ASSOCIA- TION (1909) 2010 Massachusetts Avenue, N.W. Washington, D.C. 20036 (202) 862-8330
CONTACT PERSON:	Dr. Gladys Gary Vaughn, Administrator— Research, Development and Community Rela- tions Unit (202) 862-8343
ADMINISTRATIVE UNIT:	A.H.E.A. is a national scientific and educa- tional association. Its purpose is to improve the quality of individual and family life through education, research and cooperative pro- grams.
BUDGET FY 1979–80:	Not available
STAFFING:	*PROFESSIONAL STAFF*

PROFESSIONAL STAFF
Social Work:	0
Other Social Science:	*2 Full time; 4 Part time*

STUDENTS IN TRAINING
Social Work:	0
Other Social Science:	0

RESEARCH PURPOSES/ ACTIVITIES:	To provide data for supporting systematic and long range planning of state and national Association programs; to obtain a description of the nature and extent of the home eco- nomics "outreach;" and, to help shape the goals, programs and direction of the home economics profession.
RESEARCH PRIORITIES:	*Profession Focussed:* 2, 3, 9
	Fields of Practice: 15, 19
	Special Populations: 26
	Practice Modes: 0

PUBLICATIONS

1. *Journal of Home Economics* (Quarterly)
2. *AHEA Action* (Six times per year)
3. Home Economics Research Journal (Quarterly)
4. Publications list available on request.

DATE RESEARCH UNIT
 ESTABLISHED: 1977

DIRECTORY ENTRY DATE: June, 1980

CODE NUMBER:	202073
CENTER NAME/ ADDRESS:	AMERICAN PLANNING ASSOCIATION (1978) 1776 Massachusetts Avenue, N.W. Washington, D.C. 20036 (202) 872-0611
CONTACT PERSON:	David R. Mosena, Director of Research, 1313 East 60th Street, Chicago, IL. 60637 (312) 947-2565
ADMINISTRATIVE UNIT:	The APA is a national non-profit professional and membership association serving the plan- ning field.
BUDGET FY 1979–80:	$3,000,000

STAFFING:	*PROFESSIONAL STAFF*
	  Social Work:
	  Other Social Science:
	STUDENTS IN TRAINING
	  Social Work:
	  Other Social Science:

RESEARCH PURPOSES/ ACTIVITIES:	The APA has over 40 years of experience in conducting applied research in planning and developing at the local, regional, state and national levels.

RESEARCH PRIORITIES:

Profession Focussed:	3, 5, 6, 8, 9, 10
Fields of Practice:	20, Energy
Special Populations:	All
Practice Modes:	33, 34, 35

PUBLICATIONS:	1. *PAS Memo* 2. *Land Use Law and Zoning Digest* 3. *Planning* 4. *Journal of the American Planning Association* 5. Publications list available on request.
DATE RESEARCH UNIT ESTABLISHED:	1978
DIRECTORY ENTRY DATE:	May, 1980

CODE NUMBER:	202083
CENTER NAME/ *ADDRESS:*	NATIONAL ASSOCIATION OF SOCIAL WORKERS (1955) 1425 H. Street, N.W. Washington, D.C. 20005 (202) 628-6800
CONTACT PERSON:	Leonard W. Stern A.C.S.W., Associate Executive Director (202) 628-6800
ADMINISTRATIVE UNIT:	The NASW is a national membership organization of 80,000 social workers with chapters in all 50 States and Western Europe. Research is integral to all its activities.
BUDGET FY 1979–80:	Not available
STAFFING:	*PROFESSIONAL STAFF*

PROFESSIONAL STAFF
Social Work:	9 Full time
Other Social Science:	1 Full time

STUDENTS IN TRAINING
Social Work:	3–9 per year
Other Social Science:	1–2 per year

RESEARCH PURPOSES/ *ACTIVITIES:*	The NASW engages in a broad range of research activities including labor force analyses, social policy/legislative planning studies and other studies of a special interest to the organization and its membership.
RESEARCH PRIORITIES:	*Profession Focussed:* All *Fields of Practice:* All *Special Populations:* All *Practice Modes:* All
PUBLICATIONS:	1. *Social Work* (6 times per year) 2. *Social Work Research and Abstracts* (Quarterly) 3. *Health and Social Work* (Quarterly) 4. *Social Work in Education* (Quarterly) 5. *Practice Digest* (Quarterly)

6. *The Advocate* (Periodically)
7. Publications list available on request.

DATE RESEARCH UNIT
  ESTABLISHED: 1955
DIRECTORY ENTRY DATE: June, 1980

CODE NUMBER:	202093
CENTER NAME/ ADDRESS:	AMERICAN PUBLIC HEALTH ASSOCIATION (1872) 1015 Fifteenth Street, N.W. Washington, D.C. 20005 (202) 789-5600
CONTACT PERSON:	William H. McBeath, M.D., M.P.H., Executive Director (202) 789-5600
ADMINISTRATIVE UNIT:	The APHA is a national membership organization of approximately 40,000 professionals representing all disciplines in the health field, including social work.
BUDGET FY 1979–80:	Not available
STAFFING:	*PROFESSIONAL STAFF* *Social Work:* *Other Social Science* *STUDENTS IN TRAINING* *Social Work:* *Other Social Science:*
RESEARCH PURPOSES/ ACTIVITIES:	The APHA supports a broad range of research activities in the field of public health including incidence and prevalence surveys, manpower studies, policy and legislative analyses and the like.

RESEARCH PRIORITIES:

Profession Focussed:	2, 3, 6, 7
Fields of Practice:	11, 12, 15, 16, 17, 18, 19, Public Health
Special Populations:	24, 25, 26, 27, Medically Indigent
Practice Modes:	32, 34, 35, 37

PUBLICATIONS:
1. *Journal of the American Public Health Association* (Monthly)
2. *The Nation's Health* (Monthly)
3. Publications list available on request.

DATE RESEARCH UNIT
  ESTABLISHED:
DIRECTORY ENTRY DATE: June, 1980

CODE NUMBER:	202103
CENTER NAME/ *ADDRESS:*	NATIONAL COMMITTEE AGAINST DISCRIMI- NATION IN HOUSING, INC. (1950) 1425 H. Street, N.W., Suite 410 Washington, D.C. 20005 (202) 783-8150
CONTACT PERSON:	Ernest Erber, Director of Research and Pro- gram Planning
ADMINISTRATIVE UNIT:	A national, non-profit, civil rights organization working with national and local fair housing advocacy groups to insure rights of minorities to decent housing.
BUDGET FY 1979–80:	Not available

STAFFING:	*PROFESSIONAL STAFF*
	  Social Work:
	  Other Social Science:
	STUDENTS IN TRAINING
	  Social Work:
	  Other Social Science:

RESEARCH PURPOSES/ *ACTIVITIES:*	The N.C.A.D.H. engages in research related to its organizational purpose: matters relating to equal opportunity in choice of place of res- idence for racial minorities and other social groupings.
RESEARCH PRIORITIES:	*Profession Focussed:* 1, 6, 9 *Fields of Practice:* Housing Discrimina- tion, 20, 22 *Special Populations:* 24, 25, 26, 27 *Practice Modes:* Advocacy
PUBLICATIONS:	1. *Trends in Housing* (Monthly) 2. Publications list available on request.
DATE RESEARCH UNIT *ESTABLISHED:*	1950
DIRECTORY ENTRY DATE:	March, 1980

CODE NUMBER:	202113
CENTER NAME/	
ADDRESS:	NATIONAL HOUSING CONFERENCE (1931)
	1126 16th Street, N.W.
	Washington, D.C. 20036
	(202) 223-4844
CONTACT PERSON:	Barbara Kaye, Accounts Manager
	(202) 223-4844
ADMINISTRATIVE UNIT:	The NHC is a national membership organization with specialized interests in the housing field. Research is integral to all its activities.
BUDGET FY 1979–80:	Not available
STAFFING:	*PROFESSIONAL STAFF*
	Social Work:
	Other Social Science:
	STUDENTS IN TRAINING
	Social Work:
	Other Social Science:
RESEARCH PURPOSES/	
ACTIVITIES:	The NHC engages in research related to housing policy, housing and community development legislation and housing issue analyses.
RESEARCH PRIORITIES:	*Profession Focussed:* 10
	Fields of Practice: 20
	Special Populations: 28 (Low and Moderate Income)
	Practice Modes: 35
PUBLICATIONS:	1. *Housing Yearbook* (Annual)
	2. Publications list available on request.
DATE RESEARCH UNIT	
ESTABLISHED:	1969
DIRECTORY ENTRY DATE:	June, 1980

CODE NUMBER:	202121
CENTER NAME/	
ADDRESS:	SOCIAL WORK RESEARCH CENTER
	Howard University
	School of Social Work (1940)
	Washington, DC 20059
	(202) 636-7300
CONTACT PERSON:	Dr. Alvis Adair
	(202) 636-7318
ADMINISTRATIVE UNIT:	Integral Unit of Howard University
	School of Social Work
BUDGET FY 1979–80:	$200,000

STAFFING:

PROFESSIONAL STAFF
Social Work:	3 Part time
Other Social Science:	0

STUDENTS IN TRAINING
Social Work:	2 Ph.D./D.S.W.
Other Social Science:	0

RESEARCH PURPOSES/
ACTIVITIES:

To promote empirical social work research activities among school and university faculty and students. The Center provides on-going research consultation to community health and welfare agencies.

RESEARCH PRIORITIES:
Profession Focussed:	2, 3, 8
Fields of Practice:	11, 12, 13, 15, 17, 20, 21, 22, 23
Special Populations:	
Practice Modes:	Stress management

PUBLICATIONS: 1. *Social Work Newsletter*

DATE RESEARCH UNIT
ESTABLISHED: 1973

DIRECTORY ENTRY DATE: November, 1980

CODE NUMBER: 202131/312061

CENTER NAME/
  ADDRESS: CENTER FOR THE STUDY OF SOCIAL WEL-
FARE POLICY
University of Chicago
School of Social Service Administration (1919)
236 Massachusetts Ave., N.E.
Washington, D.C. 20002
(202) 546-5062

CONTACT PERSON: Frank Farrow, Deputy Director
(202) 546-5062

ADMINISTRATIVE UNIT: Integral unit of University of Chicago School
of Social Service Administration

BUDGET FY 1979–80: $1,000,000

STAFFING:

PROFESSIONAL STAFF
  Social Work: 2 Full time
  Other Social Science: 11 Full time

STUDENTS IN TRAINING
  Social Work: 1 post-doctoral
  Other Social Science: 1 post-masters

RESEARCH PURPOSES/
  ACTIVITIES: To carry out policy analysis and research in
the areas of long term care, income support
and welfare reform, children's services and
policies, and programs for the disabled. To
provide fellowships for post-graduate students
in Washington, D.C.

RESEARCH PRIORITIES:

Profession Focussed: 2
Fields of Practice: 11, 14, 15, 16, 18, 19,
20, 22, 23
Special Populations: 24, 25, 27
Practice Modes: 35

PUBLICATIONS: 1. *Occasional Papers Series*
2. Publications list available on request.

DATE RESEARCH UNIT
  ESTABLISHED: 1979

DIRECTORY ENTRY DATE: November, 1980

CODE NUMBER: 301033

CENTER NAME/
ADDRESS: PARENTS WITHOUT PARTNERS (1957)
                         7910 Woodmont Avenue
                         Washington, D.C. 20014
                         (301) 654-8850

CONTACT PERSON: Ann Parks, Information Center
                         (301) 654-8850

ADMINISTRATIVE UNIT: PWP operates more than 1000 chapters in all
                         50 states for members. PWP is actually
                         located in Maryland, despite the District of
                         Columbia postal address.

BUDGET FY 1979–80:   Not available

STAFFING: PROFESSIONAL STAFF
                         Social Work: 0
                         Other Social Science: 2 Full time; 4 Part
                                                 time

                         STUDENTS IN TRAINING
                         Social Work: 0
                         Other Social Science: 0

RESEARCH PURPOSES/
ACTIVITIES: Research activities of the PWP are limited to
                         analysis of membership statistics and infor-
                         mal service evaluations.

RESEARCH PRIORITIES: *Profession Focussed:*   8, 9, 10
                         Fields of Practice: 15, 17
                         Special Populations: Single Parents, Chil-
                                                  dren
                         Practice Modes: 33

PUBLICATIONS: 1. *The Single Parent* (10 times per year)
                         2. Publications list available on request.

DATE RESEARCH UNIT
ESTABLISHED: 1957

DIRECTORY ENTRY DATE: June, 1980

CODE NUMBER:	404011
CENTER NAME/	
ADDRESS:	RESEARCH AND DEMONSTRATION CENTER
	School of Social Work (1920)
	Atlanta University
	223 Chestnut Street S.W.
	Atlanta, Georgia 303014
	(404) 681-0251 Ext. 262
CONTACT PERSON:	Jualynne Dodson, Director
	(404) 681-0251 Ext. 262
ADMINISTRATIVE UNIT:	Integral Unit School of Social Work, Atlanta
	University, Atlanta
BUDGET FY 1979–80:	$95,000

STAFFING:

PROFESSIONAL STAFF

Social Work:	1 Full time
Other Social Science:	1 Full time

STUDENTS IN TRAINING

Social Work:	8 Full time
Other Social Science:	0

RESEARCH PURPOSES/
ACTIVITIES:

To acquire, analyze, and employ data findings for the on-going improvement of social work education as related to Black and other oppressed communities.

RESEARCH PRIORITIES:

Profession Focussed:	3
Fields of Practice:	15, 16
Special Populations:	25, 26, 27
Practice Modes:	34, 35, 38

PUBLICATIONS: 1. Publications list available on request.

DATE RESEARCH UNIT
ESTABLISHED:

DIRECTORY ENTRY DATE: June, 1980

CODE NUMBER: 404021

CENTER NAME/
  ADDRESS;   RESEARCH INSTITUTE
                            School of Social Work (1966)
                            University of Georgia
                            Athens, Georgia 30602
                            (404) 542-3364

CONTACT PERSON: Dr. John Wodarski, Director
                            (404) 542-3364

ADMINISTRATIVE UNIT: Integral unit of University of Georgia, School
                            of Social Work

BUDGET FY 1976–77:   Not available

STAFFING: PROFESSIONAL STAFF
                            Social Work:
                            Other Social Science:
                            STUDENTS IN TRAINING
                            Social Work:
                            Other Social Science:

RESEARCH PURPOSES/
  ACTIVITIES: The Research Institute is in the process of
                            being reorganized under the leadership of a
                            new director.

RESEARCH PRIORITIES: *Profession Focussed:*
                            Fields of Practice:
                            Special Populations:
                            Practice Modes:

PUBLICATIONS: 1. Publications list available upon request.

DATE RESEARCH UNIT
  ESTABLISHED:

DIRECTORY ENTRY DATE: 1978

CODE NUMBER: 808011

CENTER NAME/
  ADDRESS: YOUTH DEVELOPMENT AND RESEARCH
CENTER
School of Social Work (1942)
University of Hawaii
2500 Campus Road
Honolulu, Hawaii 96822
(808) 948-7517

CONTACT PERSON: Jack T. Nagoshi, Director
(808) 948-7590

ADMINISTRATIVE UNIT: Integral unit of the School of Social Work,
University of Hawaii, Honolulu

BUDGET FY 1979–80: $155,000

STAFFING: PROFESSIONAL STAFF

Social Work:	1 Full time; 1 Part time
Other Social Science:	2 Full time; 6 Part time

STUDENTS IN TRAINING

Social Work:	2 Part time
Other Social Science:	0

RESEARCH PURPOSES/
  ACTIVITIES: To develop solutions for society's problems, particularly in developing alternative methods in the prevention and treatment of juvenile and youthful·offenders; to develop new knowledge through research; to stimulate faculty interest; and, to contribute to the quality of the undergraduate and graduate programs at the University.

RESEARCH PRIORITIES:
Profession Focussed:	3, 8, 9
Fields of Practice:	12, 13, 19, 23
Special Populations:	24, 25, 27 Offenders
Practice Modes:	30

PUBLICATIONS: 1. Publications list available upon request.

DATE RESEARCH UNIT
  ESTABLISHED: 1964

DIRECTORY ENTRY DATE: May, 1980

CODE NUMBER:	312011
CENTER NAME/	
ADDRESS:	JANE ADDAMS CENTER FOR SOCIAL POL-ICY AND RESEARCH
	University of Illinois at Chicago Circle (1946)
	Box 4348
	Chicago, Illinois 60680
	(312) 996-7194
CONTACT PERSON:	Dr. Shirley M. Buttrick, Director
	(312) 996-7194
ADMINISTRATIVE UNIT:	Integral Unit of Jane Addams College of Social Work, University of Illinois at Chicago Circle
BUDGET FY 1979–80:	Not available

STAFFING: *PROFESSIONAL STAFF*

Social Work:	2 Full time; 2 Part time
Other Social Science:	0

STUDENTS IN TRAINING

Social Work:	2
Other Social Science:	0

RESEARCH PURPOSES/
ACTIVITIES:

A multi-purpose research center focused on: 1) planning and evaluating programs for critical population groups; 2) designing and testing improved models of service delivery; and, 3) providing technical consultation to social welfare agencies.

RESEARCH PRIORITIES:

Profession Focussed:	5, 6, 8, 9, 10
Fields of Practice:	12, 13, 15, 16, 17
Special Populations:	24, 25, 26, 27
Practice Modes:	33, 34, 35, 37

PUBLICATIONS: 1. Publications list available on request.

DATE RESEARCH UNIT
ESTABLISHED: 1979

DIRECTORY ENTRY DATE: June, 1980

CODE NUMBER: 312021

CENTER NAME/
  ADDRESS: SOCIAL WORK RESEARCH CENTER
                          Loyola University of Chicago (1921)
                          School of Social Work
                          Chicago, Illinois 606011
                          (312) 670-3180

CONTACT PERSON: Dr. Charles Reilly, Dean
                          (312) 670-3180

ADMINISTRATIVE UNIT: When opened will be integral unit of School of
                          Social Work

BUDGET FY 1979–80:   Not applicable

STAFFING: PROFESSIONAL STAFF
                          Social Work:
                          Other Social Science:

                          STUDENTS IN TRAINING
                          Social Work:
                          Other Social Science:

RESEARCH PURPOSES/
  ACTIVITIES: To serve as a research resource to Loyola
                          University faculty, students and community
                          social agencies.

RESEARCH PRIORITIES: *Profession Focussed:*   3, 7, 9
                          Fields of Practice: 15
                          Special Populations: 27
                          Practice Modes: 30, 31

PUBLICATIONS: 1. Publications list available on request.

DATE RESEARCH UNIT
  ESTABLISHED: Scheduled to open in 1981

DIRECTORY ENTRY DATE: June, 1980

CODE NUMBER:	312033
CENTER NAME/ *ADDRESS:*	RESEARCH DEPARTMENT Public Administration Service (1933) 1776 Massachusetts Avenue, NW Washington, D.C. 20036 (202) 833-2505
CONTACT PERSON:	Jeffrey S. Slovak, Director of Research (312) 947-2132
ADMINISTRATIVE UNIT:	Public Administrative Service has a second office in Chicago, Ill. (1313 E. 60th Ave., 60637)
BUDGET FY 1979–80:	$250,000

STAFFING:

PROFESSIONAL STAFF
Social Work:	0
Other Social Science:	13 Full time; 1 Part time

STUDENTS IN TRAINING
Social Work:	0
Other Social Science:	0

RESEARCH PURPOSES/
  ACTIVITIES: PAS conducts research on questions of public administration and/or policy analysis for units of the public sector.

RESEARCH PRIORITIES:
Profession Focussed:	8, 9, 10
Fields of Practice:	Public Agency Management
Special Populations:	0
Practice Modes:	35

PUBLICATIONS: 1. Publications list available on request.

DATE RESEARCH UNIT
  ESTABLISHED: 1978

DIRECTORY ENTRY DATE: April, 1980

CODE NUMBER:	312043
CENTER NAME/	
ADDRESS:	EASTER SEAL RESEARCH FOUNDATION OF THE NATIONAL EASTER SEAL SOCIETY 2023 West Ogden Avenue Chicago, Illinois 60612 (312) 243-8400
CONTACT PERSON:	William Gellman, Ph.D., Director, Easter Seals Research Foundation (312) 321-7845
ADMINISTRATIVE UNIT:	The Foundation awards small grants to medical and behavioral scientists engaged in research on problems related to physical disability.
BUDGET FY 1979–80:	Not available

STAFFING:

PROFESSIONAL STAFF
Social Work: 0
Other Social Science: 1 Full time

STUDENTS IN TRAINING
Social Work: 0
Other Social Science: 0

RESEARCH PURPOSES/
ACTIVITIES: The objectives of the Easter Seal Research Foundation are: 1) To support applied basic and clinical research investigating the rehabilitation of crippled persons and the treatment, prevention, and cause of crippling disabilities; 2) To stimulate state and local affiliates of the rehabilitation process in measures for improving care and treatment programs; 3) To disseminate to state and local affiliates research results directly or potentially applicable to patient care service programs.

RESEARCH PRIORITIES: *Profession Focussed:*
Fields of Practice: 19
Special Populations: All
Practice Modes:

| PUBLICATIONS: | 1. *Rehabilitation Literature* (10 times per year) |
| | 2. Publications catalogue available on request. |

DATE RESEARCH UNIT
ESTABLISHED: 1956

DIRECTORY ENTRY DATE: April, 1980

CODE NUMBER:	312053
CENTER NAME/	
ADDRESS:	SOCIETY FOR HOSPITAL SOCIAL WORK DIRECTORS (1966)
	American Hospital Association
	840 North Lake Shore Drive
	Chicago, Illinois
	(312) 280-6414
CONTACT PERSON:	Salie Rossen, Society Director
	(312) 280-6414
ADMINISTRATIVE UNIT:	The Society is an integral, but financially autonomous, unit of the American Hospital Association.
BUDGET FY 1979–80:	Not available
STAFFING:	*PROFESSIONAL STAFF*

PROFESSIONAL STAFF
Social Work:	1 Full time
Other Social Science:	1 Full time

STUDENTS IN TRAININT
Social Work:	0
Other Social Science:	0

RESEARCH PURPOSES/ ACTIVITIES:

The Society limits its research to studies of manpower issues, quality control and service delivery in member hospitals and institutions. Periodic surveys are conducted, frequently through the engagement of external research contractors.

RESEARCH PRIORITIES:
Profession Focussed:	2, 3, 5, 6, 7
Fields of Practice:	16, 17, 18
Special Populations:	All
Practice Modes:	

PUBLICATIONS:

1. *Society Newsletter* (Bi-monthly)
2. *Discharge Planning Update: An Interdisciplinary Perspective* (Monthly)

DATE RESEARCH UNIT ESTABLISHED: 1966

DIRECTORY ENTRY DATE: November, 1980

CODE NUMBER:	312061/202131
CENTER NAME/	
ADDRESS:	CENTER FOR THE STUDY OF SOCIAL WEL-FARE POLICY
	University of Chicago
	School of Social Service Administration (1919
	969 East 60th Street
	Chicago, Illinois 60637
	(312) 753-4601
CONTACT PERSON:	Dr. Harold Richman, Director
	(312) 753-4633
ADMINISTRATIVE UNIT:	Integral unit of the University of Chicago
	School of Social Service Administration
BUDGET FY 1979–80:	$200,000
STAFFING:	*PROFESSIONAL STAFF*

PROFESSIONAL STAFF

Social Work:	1 Full time; 2 Part time
Other Social Science:	1 Full time; 2 Part time

STUDENTS IN TRAINING

Social Work:	8 M.A.; 1 Ph.D.
Other Social Science:	0

RESEARCH PURPOSES/
ACTIVITIES: At the present time the Center is specializing in research relating to the needs of children in Illinois. *The Children's Policy Research Project* is housed within the Center, for example, and examines a broad range of social policy and governmental administrative questions in the Child Welfare Field.

RESEARCH PRIORITIES:

Profession Focussed:	5, 7, 9, 10
Fields of Practice:	13, 14, 15, 16, 17, 18, 19, 21, 23
Special Populations:	24, 25, 26, 27
Practice Modes:	33, 34, 35, 36

PUBLICATIONS:
1. Series on Children in Illinois.
2. Publications list available on request.

DATE RESEARCH UNIT
ESTABLISHED: 1965

DIRECTORY ENTRY DATE: November, 1980

CODE NUMBER:	319011
CENTER NAME/ *ADDRESS:*	SOCIAL WORK RESEARCH CENTER University of Iowa School of Social Work 308 North Hall Iowa City, Iowa 52242 (319) 353-5255
CONTRACT PERSON:	Dr. John Craft (319) 353-7096
ADMINISTRATIVE UNIT:	University of Iowa School of Social Work.
BUDGET FY 1979–80:	Not available

STAFFING: PROFESSIONAL STAFF

Social Work:	1 Full time; 2 Part time
Other Social Science:	

STUDENTS IN TRAINING

Social Work:	10
Other Social Science:	0

RESEARCH PURPOSES/
  ACTIVITIES: The Center provides technical research consultation to social welfare agencies and University human service departments; designs and evaluates programs to improve services to critical target groups.

RESEARCH PRIORITIES:

Profession Focussed:	3, 8, 9, 10
Fields of Practice:	13, 15, 17
Special Populations:	24, 25, 26, 27
Practice Modes:	32, 33, 34, 35, 36, 37, 38

PUBLICATIONS: 1. *Child Welfare Forecasting: Content and Technique*, Charles Thomas, 1980.

DATE RESEARCH UNIT
  ESTABLISHED: 1977

DIRECTORY ENTRY DATE: July, 1980

CODE NUMBER:	502011
CENTER NAME/	
ADDRESS:	RESEARCH UNIT The Raymond A. Kent School of Social Work (1937) University of Louisville Louisville, Kentucky 40208 (502) 588-6402
CONTACT PERSON:	David S. Gochman, Ph.D., Director of Internal Research and Evaluation (502) 588-6161
ADMINISTRATIVE UNIT:	Integral Unit of School of Social Work.
BUDGET FY 1979–80:	Not available
STAFFING:	*PROFESSIONAL STAFF*

	Social Work:	0
	Other Social Science:	1 Part time

STUDENTS IN TRAINING

	Social Work:	0
	Other Social Science:	1 Part time

RESEARCH PURPOSES/	
ACTIVITIES:	To conduct research related to the education and training of graduate social work students at the University of Louisville School of Social Work.
RESEARCH PRIORITIES:	

Profession Focussed:	3
Fields of Practice:	0
Special Populations:	Students
Practice Modes:	38

PUBLICATIONS:	1. Publications list available on request.
DATE RESEARCH UNIT	
ESTABLISHED:	1973
DIRECTORY ENTRY DATE:	June, 1980

CODE NUMBER: 504011

CENTER NAME/
  ADDRESS: SOCIAL WORK RESEARCH CENTER
                            Tulane University (1927)
                            School of Social Work
                            New Orleans, Louisiana 70118
                            (504) 865-5314

CONTACT PERSON: Margaret M. Campbell, D.S.W., Director
                            Region VI Child Welfare Training Center

ADMINISTRATIVE UNIT: Center is in process of being formed. When in
                            existence, will be integral unit of School of
                            Social Work.

BUDGET FY 1979–80:   Pending

STAFFING: PROFESSIONAL STAFF
                              Social Work: 3 Part time
                              Other Social Science: 0
                            STUDENTS IN TRAINING
                              Social Work:
                              Other Social Science:

RESEARCH PURPOSES/
  ACTIVITIES: To serve as a research resource for School of
                            Social Work students, faculty and community
                            social agencies.

RESEARCH PRIORITIES: Profession Focussed: 2, 3, 7
                            Fields of Practice: 15, 16, 17, 18
                            Special Populations: 24, 25, 26, 27
                            Practice Modes: 30, 31, 38

PUBLICATIONS: 1. Publications list available on request.

DATE RESEARCH UNIT
  ESTABLISHED: Scheduled to open within near future.

DIRECTORY ENTRY DATE: June, 1980

CODE NUMBER: 504021

CENTER NAME/
  ADDRESS: SOCIAL WORK RESEARCH CENTER
Louisiana State University (1940)
School of Social Welfare
Baton Rouge, Louisiana 70803
(504) 388-5875

CONTACT PERSON: Charles Grenier, Ph.D., Research Chair
(504) 388-5875

ADMINISTRATIVE UNIT: Integral unit of School of Social Work.

BUDGET FY 1979–80: Not applicable

STAFFING:
PROFESSIONAL STAFF
  Social Work: 2 Part time
  Other Social Science: 0

STUDENTS IN TRAINING
  Social Work: 4–5
  Other Social Science: 0

RESEARCH PURPOSES/
  ACTIVITIES: To serve as research resource for faculty, students and community social agencies. The Center also will perform a research archival function.

RESEARCH PRIORITIES:
Profession Focussed: 6, 7, 8, 9
Fields of Practice:
Special Populations:
Practice Modes: 30, 31, 33, 34, 36, 37, 38

PUBLICATIONS: 1. Publications list available on request.

DATE RESEARCH UNIT
  ESTABLISHED: Center will open in 1981

DIRECTORY ENTRY DATE: June, 1980

CODE NUMBER:	301011
CENTER NAME/ ADDRESS:	RESEARCH CENTER School of Social Work and Community Planning (1963) University of Maryland 525 Redwood Street Baltimore, Maryland 21201 (301) 528-5125
CONTACT PERSON:	Jerry S. Turem, Ph.D., Director (301) 528-5125
ADMINISTRATIVE UNIT:	Integral unit of the School of Social Work and Community Planning, University of Maryland, Baltimore.
BUDGET FY 1979–80:	$150,000

STAFFING:

PROFESSIONAL STAFF

Social Work:	0 Full time; 2 Part time
Other Social Science:	2 Full time; 2 Part time

STUDENTS IN TRAINING

Social Work:	1 Full time; 22 Part time
Other Social Science:	0

RESEARCH PURPOSES/ ACTIVITIES:

The Center primarily engages in state-sponsored Department of Public Welfare research in the areas of gerontology, deviance, adolescence, health, mental health, and utilization of human services. Seeks small faculty/student projects as well as federally funded research in areas of interest to staff. Establishing a teaching/learning center for practice research.

RESEARCH PRIORITIES:

Profession Focussed:	5, 8, 9
Fields of Practice:	11, 12, 13, 14, 15, 16, 17
Special Populations:	27, 28
Practice Modes:	0

PUBLICATIONS: 1. Publications list available on request.

DATE RESEARCH UNIT
  ESTABLISHED: 1977

DIRECTORY ENTRY DATE: June, 1980

CODE NUMBER: 301023

CENTER NAME/
ADDRESS: AMERICAN CORRECTIONAL ASSOCIATION
(1870)
4321 Hartwick Road, Suite 319
College Park, Maryland 20740
(301) 864-1070

CONTACT PERSON: Jay Worrall, Program Manager
(301) 699-7600

ADMINISTRATIVE UNIT: The ACA organization includes state chapters
and affiliate organizations.

BUDGET FY 1979–80 ACA = $1,000,000

STAFFING PROFESSIONAL STAFF
Social Work: 0
Other Social Science: 13

STUDENTS IN TRAINING
Social Work: 0
Other Social Science: 0

RESEARCH PURPOSES
ACTIVITIES: The ACA, from time to time, undertakes specialized studies related to its special purpose,
i.e., representation of the field of corrections
on the national level and to promote its
advancement.

RESEARCH PRIORITIES:
Profession Focussed: 2, 3, 7
Fields of Practice: 11, 12, 13, 23
Special Populations: Professionals in Cor-
rections; Inmates and
clients
Practice Modes: 33, 34, 35, 37

PUBLICATIONS: 1. Publicatons list available on request.

DATE RESEARCH UNIT
ESTABLISHED:

DIRECTORY ENTRY DATE: June, 1980

CODE NUMBER: 413011

CENTER NAME/
ADDRESS: RESEARCH CENTER
Smith College (1919)
School for Social Work
Northampton, Massachusetts 01063
(413) 584-2700 Ext. 2104

CONTACT PERSON: Dr. Angelika Robertson, Research Associate
(413) 584-2700 Ext. 2104

ADMINISTRATIVE UNIT: Integral unit of Smith College School for
Social Work.

BUDGET FY 1979–80: Not available.

STAFFING: PROFESSIONAL STAFF
Social Work: 1 Part time
Other Social Science: 1 Full time
STUDENTS IN TRAINING
Social Work:
Other Social Science:

RESEARCH PURPOSES/
ACTIVITIES: To facilitate clinical social work research. Pro
jects include research on the educational pro
cess, clinical interaction, delivery systems
and aspects of client and/or worker systems
social policy issues, history of the profession
and evaluation.

RESEARCH PRIORITIES: *Profession Focused:* 1, 3
Fields of Practice: 11, 15, 17
Special Populations: *25, 26*
Practice Modes: 30, 36 Clinical Social
Work Practice

PUBLICATIONS: 1. *Smith College Studies in Social Work* (Qua
terly)

DATE RESEARCH UNIT
ESTABLISHED: 1977

DIRECTORY ENTRY DATE: June, 1980

CODE NUMBER: 617011

CENTER NAME/
ADDRESS: SCHOOL OF SOCIAL WORK (1939)
Boston University
264 Bay State Road
Boston, Massachusetts 02215
(617) 353-3750

CONTACT PERSON: Dr. Clarence Sherwood, Chair Research
Sequence
(617) 353-3748

ADMINISTRATIVE UNIT: Research activities are integrated into on-
going faculty responsibilities. No formally
organized/named center/institute as such.

BUDGET FY 1979–80: $275,000

STAFFING: PROFESSIONAL STAFF
Social Work: 1 Full time; 2 Part
time
Other Social Science: 3 Full time; 2 Part
time

STUDENTS IN TRAINING
Social Work: 15 M.S.W.
Other Social Science: 3 undergraduate

RESEARCH PURPOSES/
ACTIVITIES: To provide institutional support for faculty and
staff engaged in social work research; to provide practical research training for students
in social work.

RESEARCH PRIORITIES: Profession Focussed: 2, 5, 8, 9, 10
Fields of Practice: 11, 16, 17, 18, 19, 20
Special Populations:
Practice Modes:

PUBLICATONS: 1. Publications list available on request.

DATE RESEARCH UNIT
ESTABLISHED: 1979

DIRECTORY ENTRY DATE: November, 1980

CODE NUMBER:	617021
CENTER NAME/ *ADDRESS:*	LEVINSON POLICY INSTITUTE Brandeis University Heller Graduate School Waltham, Massachusetts 02254 (617) 647-2928
CONTACT PERSON:	Dr. James Callahan, Director (617) 647-2173
ADMINISTRATIVE UNIT:	The Institute is an integral unit of the Heller Graduate School for Advanced Studies in Social Welfare.
BUDGET FY 1979–80:	$1,671,000

STAFFING

PROFESSIONAL STAFF

Social Work:	1 Full time; 1 Part time
Other Social Science:	6 Full time; 1 Part time

STUDENTS IN TRAINING

Social Work:	1 Ph.D.
Other Social Science:	6 Undergraduates

RESEARCH PURPOSES/ *ACTIVITIES:*	The Policy Institute focuses research on long term disability problems of persons of all age groups. Presently, the Institute is providing leadership in the study of "social and health maintenance organizations" (SHMO's).

RESEARCH PRIORITIES:

Profession Focussed:	
Fields of Practice:	16, 17, 18, 19
Special Populations:	28a, 28b
Practice Modes:	35

PUBLICATIONS:	1. The Institute publishes a *Monograph Series* 2. Publications list available on request.
DATE RESEARCH UNIT *ESTABLISHED:*	1968
DIRECTORY ENTRY DATE:	November, 1980

CODE NUMBER:	617031
CENTER NAME/ ADDRESS:	CENTER FOR EMPLOYMENT AND INCOME STUDIES Brandeis University Heller Graduate School Waltham, Massachusetts 02254 (617) 647-2928
CONTACT PERSON:	Dr. Leonard Hausman, Director (617) 647-2936
ADMINISTRATIVE UNIT:	The Center is an integral unit of the Heller Graduate School for Advanced Studies in Social Welfare.
BUDGET FY 1979–80:	$1,110,000

STAFFING:

PROFESSIONAL STAFF

Social Work:	2 Full time; 1 Part time
Other Social Science:	12 Full time; 4 Part time

STUDENTS IN TRAINING

Social Work:	6 Ph.D.
Other Social Science:	0

RESEARCH PURPOSES/ ACTIVITIES: At the present time, the Center devotes most of its resources to studies related to federally financed youth education and food stamp programs.

RESEARCH PRIORITIES:

Profession Focussed:	
Fields of Practice:	14, 16, 23
Special Populations:	24, 25, 26, 27
Practice Modes:	35

PUBLICATIONS: 1. *CEIS Newsletter* (Quarterly)
2. Publications list available on request.

DATE RESEARCH UNIT ESTABLISHED: 1979

DIRECTORY ENTRY DATE: November, 1980

CODE NUMBER:	617041
CENTER NAME/ *ADDRESS:*	NATIONAL AGING POLICY CENTER ON INCOME MAINTENANCE Brandeis University Heller Graduate School Waltham, Massachusetts 02254 (617) 647-2928
CONTACT PERSON:	Dr. Robert Binstock, Director (617) 647-2912
ADMINISTRATIVE UNIT:	The Center is an integral unit of the Heller Graduate School for Advanced Studies in Social Welfare
BUDGET FY 1979–80:	$400,000
STAFFING:	*PROFESSIONAL STAFF*

Social Work: 0
Other Social Science: 5 Full time; 15 Part time

STUDENTS IN TRAINING
Social Work: 15 Ph.D.
Other Social Science:

RESEARCH PURPOSES/ *ACTIVITIES:*	The NAPC engages in research on pensions and the income maintenance needs of retirees.

RESEARCH PRIORITIES: *Profession Focussed:*
Fields of Practice: 11, 14, 23
Special Populations: Aged
Practice Modes: 35

PUBLICATIONS:	1. Publications list available on request.
DATE RESEARCH UNIT *ESTABLISHED:*	1980
DIRECTORY ENTRY DATE:	November, 1980

CODE NUMBER: 617051

CENTER NAME/
  ADDRESS: CENTER FOR HEALTH POLICY ANALYSIS
AND RESEARCH
Brandeis University
Heller Graduate School
Waltham, Massachusetts 02254
(617) 647-2928

CONTACT PERSON: Dr. Stanley Wallack
(617) 647-2895

ADMINISTRATIVE UNIT: The Center is an integral unit of the Heller
Graduate School for Advanced Studies in
Social Welfare

BUDGET FY 1979–80: $1,230,000

STAFFING: PROFESSIONAL STAFF

Social Work:	3 Full time
Other Social Science:	8 Full time; 1 Part time

STUDENTS IN TRAINING

Social Work:	7 Ph.D.
Other Social Science:	

RESEARCH PURPOSES/
  ACTIVITIES: The Center emphasizes social policy research
on long term care in the field of health, health
programs, and health maintenance organizations.

RESEARCH PRIORITIES:
Profession Focussed:

Fields of Practice:	16, 17
Special Populations:	Physically and Emo-tionally Ill
Practice Modes:	35

PUBLICATIONS: 1. *Update* (Monthly
2. *Book Series*
3. *Working Paper Series*
4. Publications list available on request.

DATE RESEARCH UNIT
  ESTABLISHED: 1978

DIRECTORY ENTRY DATE: November, 1980

CODE NUMBER:	218011
CENTER NAME/	
ADDRESS:	CENTER FOR RESEARCH, EVALUATION, TRAINING
	School of Social Development (1973)
	University of Minnesota
	Duluth, Minnesota 55812
	(218) 726-7961
CONTACT PERSON:	Irl Carter, Dean
	(218) 726-7245, ext. 30
ADMINISTRATIVE UNIT:	Integral unit of the School of Social Development, University of Minnesota, Duluth.
BUDGET FY 1976–77:	$24,000

STAFFING:

PROFESSIONAL STAFF

Social Work:	7 Full time
Other Social Science:	0

STUDENTS IN TRAINING

Social Work:	1 MSW
Other Social Science:	0

*RESEARCH PURPOSES/
ACTIVITIES:*

To conduct applied research in the form of evaluations, needs assessments, etc., in conjunction with the Center's training projects; and, to provide consultation in setting up management information systems.

RESEARCH PRIORITIES:

Profession Focussed:	
Fields of Practice:	11, 12, 13, 15, 17, 23
Special Populations:	25, 27 American Indians
Practice Modes:	32, 33, 34, 35, 36, 37

PUBLICATONS:	1. Publications list available on request.
DATE RESEARCH UNIT ESTABLISHED:	1976
DIRECTORY ENTRY DATE:	June, 1980

CODE NUMBER: 601011

CENTER NAME/
  ADDRESS: SOCIAL WORK RESEARCH INSTITUTE
University of Southern Mississippi
School of Social Work (1974)
Southern Station Box 5114
Hattiesburg, Mississippi 39401
(601) 266-4201

CONTACT PERSON: Jerome Zimmerman, Ph.D., Director

ADMINISTRATIVE UNIT: The Institute is an integral unit of the University of Southern Mississippi School of Social Work.

BUDGET FY 1979–80: $30,000

STAFFING: *PROFESSIONAL STAFF*
    Social Work: 1 Part time
    Other Social Science: 0

  STUDENTS IN TRAINING
    Social Work: 30 M.S.W.
    Other Social Science: 0

RESEARCH PURPOSES/
  ACTIVITIES: The Institute seeks to encourage and support research in the social services primarily for concerns of the state of Mississippi. Provides research technical assistance and consultation to various state and private human service agencies.

RESEARCH PRIORITIES: *Profession Focussed:*   2, 3, 5, 6, 7, 8, 9
  Fields of Practice: 11, 14, 15, 16 17, 20, 22, 23

  Special Populations: All
  Practice Modes: 30, 31, 32, 33, 34, 35, 36

PUBLICATIONS: 1. Publications list available on request.

DATE RESEARCH UNIT
  ESTABLISHED: 1980

DIRECTORY ENTRY DATE: June, 1980

CODE NUMBER:	201011
CENTER NAME/	
ADDRESS:	SOCIAL WORK RESEARCH CENTER
	Graduate School of Social Work (1957)
	Rutgers University
	New Brunswick, New Jersey 08903
	(201) 932-7114
CONTACT PERSON:	Dr. Ludwig L. Geismar, Director
	(201) 932-7114
ADMINISTRATIVE UNIT:	Integral unit of the School of Social Work, Rutgers University, New Brunswick.
BUDGET FY 1979–80:	Not available

STAFFING:

PROFESSIONAL STAFF

Social Work:	6 Part time
Other Social Science:	1 Full time; 2 Part time

STUDENTS IN TRAINING

Social Work:	2 Part time
Other Social Science:	0

RESEARCH PURPOSES/
  ACTIVITIES: The provision of a structure for social work research aimed at developing and expanding knowledge consistent with the goals of the profession; the stimulation of research training of graduate students; and the provision of facilities and technical consultation to faculty in their own research activities.

RESEARCH PRIORITIES:

Profession Focussed:	2, 7
Fields of Practice:	11, 12, 13, 15, 16, 17
Special Populations:	24, 25, 26, 27
Practice Modes:	30, 31, 33, 35

PUBLICATIONS: 1. Reprint list available on request.

DATE RESEARCH UNIT
  ESTABLISHED: 1965

DIRECTORY ENTRY DATE: May, 1980

CODE NUMBER: 201022

CENTER NAME/
ADDRESS: CENTER FOR INTERNATIONAL AND COM-
PARATIVE SOCIAL WELFARE
Rutgers University
International Studies Center
180 College Avenue
New Brunswick, New Jersey 08903
(201) 932-7263

CONTACT PERSON: Dr. Werner W. Boehm, Director
(201) 932-7263

ADMINISTRATIVE UNIT: Integral unit of Rutgers University; works
cooperatively with the School of Social Work
and other Social Science Departments of the
University.

BUDGET FY 1979–80: $10,000

STAFFING: *PROFESSIONAL STAFF*
   Social Work: 1 Part time
   Other Social Science: 0

  STUDENTS IN TRAINING
   Social Work: 0
   Other Social Science: 0

RESEARCH PURPOSES/
ACTIVITIES: Coordination and exchange of information, lit-
erature collection; clearinghouse function;
workshops and seminars.

RESEARCH PRIORITIES: *Profession Focussed:* 2, 3, 8
Fields of Practice: International Social
Welfare

Special Populations:
Practice Modes:

PUBLICATIONS: 1. Publications list available on request.

DATE RESEARCH UNIT
ESTABLISHED: 1973

DIRECTORY ENTRY DATE: June, 1980

CODE NUMBER:	212011
CENTER NAME/ ADDRESS:	RESEARCH CENTER Graduate School of Social Service (1929) Fordham University of Lincoln Center New York, New York 10023 (212) 841-5526
CONTACT PERSON:	Dr. Eugene Shinn, Director (212) 841-5526
ADMINISTRATIVE UNIT:	Integral unit of the Fordham University at Lincoln Center School of Social Service.
BUDGET FY 1976–77:	Not available

STAFFING:

PROFESSIONAL STAFF

Social Work:	4 Full time; 3 Part time
Other Social Science:	3 Full time

STUDENTS IN TRAINING

Social Work:	6 Part time
Other Social Science:	10 Part time

RESEARCH PURPOSES/ ACTIVITIES:

To offer consultations to agencies seeking help in proposal writing and development of research activities in general. To provide research and proposal writing consultation to faculty, colleagues, and to involve students and faculty in school-based research.
The center also conducts research contributing to knowledge and practice in the profession.

RESEARCH PRIORITIES:

Profession Focussed:	3
Fields of Practice:	11, 14, 15
Special Populations:	24, 25, 26, 27
Practice Modes:	All

PUBLICATIONS: 1. Publications list available on request.

DATE RESEARCH UNIT ESTABLISHED:

DIRECTORY ENTRY DATE: 1978

CODE NUMBER: 212023

CENTER NAME/
 ADDRESS: DATA CENTER, NATIONAL BOARD
                             Young Women's Christian Association (1855)
                             600 Lexington Avenue
                             New York, New York 10022
                             (212) 753-4700

CONTACT PERSON: Alice Levine, Executive, Data Center
                             (212) 753-4700

ADMINISTRATIVE UNIT: Research unit of the National board of the
                             YWCA of the United States.

BUDGET FY 1979–80:   Not available

STAFFING: PROFESSIONAL STAFF
                               Social Work: N/A
                               Other Social Science:

                             STUDENTS IN TRAINING
                               Social Work: N/A
                               Other Social Science:

RESEARCH PURPOSES/
 ACTIVITIES: Engages in action-oriented research of inter-
                             est to the YWCA including local and national
                             needs, assessment studies, surveys and
                             organization-related research.

RESEACH PRIORITIES: Profession Focussed: 8, 9
                             Fields of Practice: 15, Youth Develop-
                                                     ment and Enrichment
                             Special Populations: 24, 25, 26, 27
                             Practice Modes: 31, 32

PUBLICATIONS: 1. *The Printout*, Participation data (Annually)

DATE RESEARCH UNIT
 ESTABLISHED: 1970

DIRECTORY ENTRY DATE: May, 1980

CODE NUMBER:	212033
CENTER NAME/	
ADDRESS:	THE FLORENCE G. HELLER—JWB RESEARCH CENTER
	15 East 26th Street
	New York, New York 10010
	(212) 532-4949
CONTACT PERSON:	Dr. S. Morton Altman, Director
ADMINISTRATIVE UNIT:	JWB Center is in the process of reorganization.
BUDGET FY 1979–80:	Not available
STAFFING:	*PROFESSIONAL STAFF*
	Social Work: 1 Full time; several Part time
	Other Social Science:
	STUDENTS IN TRAINING
	Social Work:
	Other Social Science:
RESEARCH PURPOSES/	
ACTIVITIES:	The development of short-term practice oriented research that has relevance to evaluating the effectiveness of programs of Jewish Community Centers and other similar organizations.
RESEARCH PRIORITIES:	*Profession Focussed:* 8, 9
	Fields of Practice: Jewish Comunal Service, 15
	Special Populations: 24, 25, 26, 27, Aged
	Practice Modes: 30, 31, 32
PUBLICATIONS:	1. *Research Digest* (Monograph Series)
	2. List available upon request.
DATE RESEARCH UNIT	
ESTABLISHED:	
DIRECTORY ENTRY DATE:	May, 1980

CODE NUMBER:	212043
CENTER NAME/ *ADDRESS:*	NATIONAL ASSOCIATION FOR THE ADVANCEMENT OF COLORED PEOPLE (1909) 1790 Broadway New York, New York 10019 (212) 245-2100
CONTACT PERSON:	Michael Meyers, Assistant Director
ADMINISTRATIVE UNIT:	Research is an integral part of all NAACP activities.
BUDGET FY 1979–80:	NAACP = $3,351,000

STAFFING:	*PROFESSIONAL STAFF*
	  Social Work:
	  Other Social Science:

	STUDENTS IN TRAINING Many full and part time
	  Social Work:
	  Other Social Science:

RESEARCH PURPOSES/ *ACTIVITIES:*	To conduct research on all issues pertaining to the civil rights and advancement of peoples of color.
RESEARCH PRIORITIES:	*Profession Focussed:* 8, 9 *Fields of Practice:* 14, 20, 22, 23 *Special Populations:* 25 *Practice Modes:* All
PUBLICATIONS:	1. *Annual Report* and selected publications.
DATE RESEARCH UNIT *ESTABLISHED:*	1909
DIRECTORY ENTRY DATE:	May, 1980

CODE NUMBER:	212053
CENTER NAME/ *ADDRESS:*	UNITED NEIGHBORHOOD CENTERS OF AMERICA, INC. (1911) 232 Madison Avenue New York, New York 10016 (212) 679-6110
CONTACT PERSON:	Inez L. Almond, Director of Public Relations
ADMINISTRATIVE UNIT:	Formerly known as the National Federation of Settlements, UNCA is a voluntary, non-profit agency with 140 members which operate 360 Centers in 80 cities and 30 states.
BUDGET FY 1979–80:	$45,000

STAFFING

PROFESSIONAL STAFF
Social Work:	3 Full time; 1 Part time
Other Social Science:	2 Full time

STUDENTS IN TRAINING
Social Work:	0
Other Social Science:	0

RESEARCH PURPOSES/ *ACTIVITIES:*	Though UNCA does not have a formally structured research unit, the agency does gather and disseminate descriptive statistics concerning member agency activities on a regular basis; also conducts special purpose studies.

RESEARCH PRIORITIES:
Profession Focussed:	3, 6, 7
Fields of Practice:	11, 13, 15, 20, 22, 23
Special Populations:	24, 25, 26, 27
Practice Modes:	31

PUBLICATIONS:	1. Publications list available on request.
DATE RESEARCH UNIT *ESTABLISHED:*	1911
DIRECTORY ENTRY DATE:	May, 1980

CODE NUMBER:	212063
CENTER NAME/	
ADDRESS:	NATIONAL CHILD LABOR COMMITTEE (1904)
	1501 Broadway, Room 1111
	New York, New York 10036
	(212) 840-1801
CONTACT PERSON:	Dr. Rae Weissman, Research Associate
	(212) 840-1801
ADMINISTRATIVE UNIT:	The NCLC works to protect and promote the rights of children and youth as they pertain to work and working.
BUDGET FY 1979–80:	$100,000

STAFFING:

PROFESSIONAL STAFF

Social Work:	1 Full time; 1 Part time
Other Social Science:	6 Full time; 1 Part time

STUDENTS IN TRAINING

Social Work:	0
Other Social Science;	0

RESEARCH PURPOSES/
  ACTIVITIES: The NCLC's research staff supports the primary organizing purpose of the organization through studies and evaluations of various types.

RESEARCH PRIORITIES:

Profession Focussed:	2, 3, 9
Fields of Practice:	15, 17, 21, 23
Special Populations:	24, 25, 27, Paraprofessionals
Practice Modes:	0

PUBLICATIONS: 1. *New Generations* (Quarterly)

DATE RESEARCH UNIT
  ESTABLISHED: 1904

DIRECTORY ENTRY DATE: May, 1980

CODE NUMBER:	212073
CENTER NAME/ ADDRESS;	RESEARCH DEPARTMENT Family Service Association of America (1911) 44 East 23rd Street New York, New York 10010 (212) 674-6100
CONTACT PERSON:	Dorothy Fahs Beck, Ph.D., Director of Research (212) 674-6100, Ext. 29
ADMINISTRATIVE UNIT:	FSAA research occurs in three organizational units: Research Department; Division of Information Systems and Services Purposes; and, Division of Policy Analysis and Development Purpose.
BUDGET FY 1979–80:	$80,000

STAFFING:

PROFESSIONAL STAFF
Social Work: 1 Part time
Other Social Science: 1 Full time; 3 Part time

STUDENTS IN TRAINING
Social Work 0
Other Social Science: 0

RESEARCH PURPOSES/ ACTIVITIES:

To promote and support basic knowledge building and improve service evaluation in the family service field; to serve the informational needs of the family service field; to improve administrative planning and to facilitate the formulation of private and public policies on the family on the basis of appropriate data.

RESEARCH PRIORITIES:

Profession Focussed: 2, 3, 5, 8, 9, 10
Fields of Practice: 15, Family Life Education
Special Populations: 24, 25, 27
Practice Modes: 30, 34, 35, 36, 38

PUBLICATIONS:

1. *Family Service Profiles* (3 issues per year)
2. *Family Listening Post* (Biennial)
3. *Unit Cost Exchange* (Annual)
4. Publications list available on request.

DATE RESEARCH UNIT
  ESTABLISHED: 1955
DIRECTORY ENTRY DATE: June, 1980

CODE NUMBER:	212083
CENTER NAME/ *ADDRESS:*	NATIONAL COUNCIL FOR HOMEMAKER- HOME HEALTH AIDE SERVICES, INC. (1962) 67 Irving Place New York, New York 10003 (212) 674-4990
CONTACT PERSON:	Dr. Eugene Shinn, Research Consultant (212) 674-4990
ADMINISTRATIVE UNIT:	Research is conducted on a contractual basis with area research facilities.
BUDGET FY 1979–80:	$10,000
STAFFING:	*PROFESSIONAL STAFF*

PROFESSIONAL STAFF
Social Work:	2 Part time
Other Social Science:	0

STUDENTS IN TRAINING
Social Work:	1 M.S.W.; 1 D.S.W.
Other Social Science:	0

RESEARCH PRUPOSES/
ACTIVITIES: To conduct basic research to increase knowledge base and for developing standards in homemaker-home health aide services; to conduct evaluations of the Council's demonstration and other projects; to conduct fact-finding surveys for planning and policy activities at the Council.

RESEARCH PRIORITIES:
Profession Focussed:	3, 7
Fields of Practice:	11, Homemaker- Health Services
Special Populations:	Disabled, Cronically ill
Practice Modes:	0

PUBLICATIONS: 1. Publications list available on request.

DATE RESEARCH UNIT
ESTABLISHED: 1971

DIRECTORY ENTRY DATE: March, 1980

CODE NUMBER:	212093
CENTER NAME/ *ADDRESS:*	CONGRESS ON RACIAL EQUALITY (1942) 1916–38 Park Avenue New York, New York 10037 (212) 690-3678
CONTACT PERSON:	Mr. George Holmes, Communications Coordinator (212) 690-3678
ADMINISTRATIVE UNIT:	Research is integral to all C.O.R.E. activities.
BUDGET FY 1979–80:	$250,000

STAFFING:

PROFESSIONAL STAFF

Social Work:	9 Full time; 1 Part time
Other Social Science:	3 Full time; 1 Part time

STUDENTS IN TRAINING

Social Work:	1 M.S.W.; Several doctoral
Other Social Science:	Several doctoral

RESEARCH PURPOSES/
  ACTIVITIES:

To investigate and interpret civil rights laws and policies of the government and private corporations. Also examines and consults on affirmative action programs and conducts research relevant seminars.

RESEARCH PRIORITIES:

Profession Focussed:	3, 6
Fileds of Practice:	11, 12, 13, 14, 15, 16, 17, 18, 19, 20, 21, 22, 23
Special Populations:	24, 25, 26, 27
Practice Modes:	32, 34, 37, 38

PUBLICATIONS:

1. *CORE Magazine* (Quarterly)
2. *CORE Equal Opportunity Journal* (4–6 times yearly)
3. *CORELATOR* (Monthly)
4. Publications list available on request.

DATE RESEARCH UNIT *ESTABLISHED:*	1945
DIRECTORY ENTRY DATE:	March, 1980.

CODE NUMBER:	212103
CENTER NAME/ ADDRESS:	RESEARCH CENTER Child Welfare League of America (1920) 67 Irving Place New York, New York 10003 (212) 254-7410
CONTACT PERSON:	Mary Ann Jones, Director of Research (212) 254-7410, Ext. 301
ADMINISTRATIVE UNIT:	CWLA is a national membership organization consisting of approximately 400 Child Welfare Agencies.
BUDGET FY 1979–80:	$378,000

STAFFING:

PROFESSIONAL STAFF

Social Work:	2 Full time; 1 Part time
Other Social Science:	4 Full time; 2 Part time

STUDENTS IN TRAINING

Social Work:	0
Other Social Science:	0

RESEARCH PURPOSES/ ACTIVITIES:

The Research Center conducts publicly and privately funded research and evaluation studies in the areas of childbearing, foster care, preventive services, child abuse and neglect, and adoption. In addition, the Center provides League member agencies with surveys of trends in programs, staff salaries, and sources of agency income.

RESEARCH PRIORITIES:

Profession Focussed:	7, 8, 9
Fields of Practice:	15, 16, 17, 18, 19, 20
Special Populations:	24, 25, 26, 27
Practice Modes:	30, 31

PUBLICATIONS:

1. Extensive publications list available upon request.

DATE RESEARCH UNIT ESTABLISHED:	1955
DIRECTORY ENTRY DATE:	June, 1980

CODE NUMBER:	212113
CENTER NAME/ *ADDRESS:*	COUNCIL ON SOCIAL WORK EDUCATION (1952) 111 Eighth Avenue New York, New York 10011 (212) 242-3800
CONTACT PERSON:	Dr. Arthur Katz, Executive Director (212) 242-3800
ADMINISTRATIVE UNIT:	The CSWE is a national membership organization of approximately 3000 social work educators, agency administrators, universities, undergraduate and graduate schools of social work.
BUDGET FY 1979–80:	CSWE = $902,608

STAFFING:	*PROFESSIONAL STAFF*
	    Social Work:
	    Other Social Science:
	STUDENTS IN TRAINING
	    Social Work:
	    Other Social Science:

RESEARCH PURPOSES/ *ACTIVITIES:*	CSWE collects on-going statistics regarding application, admission and matriculation of students to graduate and undergraduate schools of social work. Manpower studies and other projects of interest to the Council's membership are conducted regularly.
RESEARCH PRIORITIES:	*Profession Focussed:* 2, 3, 5, 7, 8 *Fields of Practice:* All *Special Populations:* All *Practice Modes:* All
PUBLICATIONS:	1. *Statistics on Social Work Education* (Annual) 2. *Journal of Social Work Education* (Quarterly) 3. Publications list available on request.
DATE RESEARCH UNIT *ESTABLISHED:*	1952
DIRECTORY ENTRY DATE:	June, 1980

CODE NUMBER:	212123
CENTER NAME/ *ADDRESS:*	GIRL SCOUTS OF THE U.S.A. (1912) 830 Third Avenue New York, New York 10022 (212) 940-7500
CONTACT PERSON:	Mrs. D. Selzer, Director for Research and Analysis (212) 940-7674
ADMINISTRATIVE UNIT:	The Girl Scouts of the U.S.A. has approximately 2,500,500 girls in programs in all states.
BUDGET FY 1979–80:	Not available.

STAFFING:	*PROFESSIONAL STAFF*
	  Social Work:
	  Other Social Science:
	
	STUDENTS IN TRAINING
	  Social Work:
	  Other Social Science:

RESEARCH PURPOSES/ *ACTIVITIES:*	The Girl Scouts engages primarily in research related to the special need of girls 6–17, internal administrative analyses, membership statistical analyses, and other studies of interest to the organization.

RESEARCH PRIORITIES:

Profession Focussed:	2, 3, 4, 8, 9, 10
Fields of Practice:	15, 21
Special Populations:	24, 25, Girls ages 6–17, 26
Practice Modes:	

PUBLICATIONS:	1. *The Leader* (9 times per year) 2. *Daisy* (9 times per year) 3. Publications list available on request.
DATE RESEARCH UNIT *ESTABLISHED:*	
DIRECTORY ENTRY DATE:	June, 1980

CODE NUMBER:	212133
CENTER NAME/ *ADDRESS:*	AMERICAN FOUNDATION FOR THE BLIND (1921) 15 West 16th Street New York, New York 10011 (212) 620-2000
CONTACT PERSON:	Corinne Kirchner, Director of Social Research (212) 620-2067
ADMINISTRATIVE UNIT:	A national organization providing consultation, social research, professional publications and public education, technological research and adapted products for visually impaired persons.
BUDGET FY 1979–80:	Not provided.
STAFFING:	PROFESSIONAL STAFF *Social Work:* *Other Social Science:* STUDENTS IN TRAINING *Social Work:* *Other Social Science:*
RESEARCH PURPOSES/ *ACTIVITIES:*	The AFB engages in research on the prevalence, demography and social description of visually impaired and blind persons.

RESEARCH PRIORITIES:

Profession Focussed:	8, 9
Fields of Practice:	19, Visually impaired
Special Populations:	Visually impaired
Practice Modes:	31, 35

PUBLICATIONS:	1. *Journal of Visual Impairment and Blindness* (Monthly) 2. Publications catalogue available on request.
DATE RESEARCH UNIT *ESTABLISHED:*	1921
DIRECTORY ENTRY DATE:	June, 1980

CODE NUMBER: 212151

CENTER NAME/
  ADDRESS: RESEARCH AND DEMONSTRATION CENTER
                      Columbia University
                      School of Social Work (1919)
                      622 West 113th Street
                      New York, New York 10025
                      (212) 280-4088

CONTACT PERSON: Dr. David Fanshell, Director
                      (212) 280-3250

ADMINISTRATIVE UNIT: Integral unit of the Columbia University
                      School of Social Work.

BUDGET FY 1979–80: $1,200,000

STAFFING: PROFESSIONAL STAFF
                        Social Work: 18 Full time; 9 Part
                                            time
                        Other Social Science: 9 Full time; 4 Part
                                            time

                      STUDENTS IN TRAINING
                        Social Work: 18 M.S.W.; 6 D.S.W.
                        Other Social Science: 3 Ph.D.

RESEARCH PURPOSES/
  ACTIVITIES: The Center engages in a broad range of
                      research focussed on the improvement of
                      social work services and the service delivery
                      system. Provides research consultation and
                      assistance to University students and faculty
                      as well as community social and health agen-
                      cies.

RESEARCH PRIORITIES: Profession Focussed: 2, 3, 4, 5, 8, 9
                      Fields of Practice: 11, 12, 13, 14, 15, 16
                                             17, 19, 20, 23e
                      Special Populations: 24, 25, 26, 27, Indus-
                                             trial Workers
                      Practice Modes: All

PUBLICATIONS: 1. Publications list available on request.

DATE RESEARCH UNIT
  ESTABLISHED: 1958

DIRECTORY ENTRY DATE: November, 1980

CODE NUMBER:	516011
CENTER NAME/	
ADDRESS:	ADELPHI UNIVERSITY
	School of Social Work (1955)
	Garden City, Long Island, New York 11530
	(516) 560-8118
CONTACT PERSON:	Ralph Dolgoff, D.S.W., Assistant Dean for Academic Affairs
	(516) 560-8118
ADMINISTRATIVE UNIT:	Research within the School is decentralized into the following units: Center for Social Policy; Social Work Service Center; Institute for Child Mental Health; field instruction division; and, Doctoral Program.
BUDGET FY 1979–80:	Not available.
STAFFING:	*PROFESSIONAL STAFF*

STAFFING continued:

	Social Work:	4 Full time; 10 Part time
	Other Social Science:	4 Full time
	STUDENTS IN TRAINING	
	Social Work:	Many
	Other Social Science:	

RESEARCH PURPOSES/	
ACTIVITIES:	Conduct social research to improve excellence of practice, delivery of services, social work educational curriculum and organization in unemployment, mental health, women's issues.
RESEARCH PRIORITIES:	*Profession Focussed:* 3, 5, 7, 8, 9
	Fields of Practice: 11, 12, 13, 14, 15, 16, 17, 18, 19, 20, 21, 22, 23, Rural Social Work
	Special Populations: 24, 25, 26, 27
	Practice Modes: 30, 31, 32, 33, 38
PUBLICATIONS:	1. Publications list available upon request.
DATE RESEARCH UNIT	
ESTABLISHED:	
DIRECTORY ENTRY DATE:	June, 1980

CODE NUMBER:	914013
CENTER NAME/	
ADDRESS:	THE INSTITUTE FOR SOCIOECONOMIC STUDIES
	Airport Road
	White Plains, New York 10604
	(914) 428-7400
CONTACT PERSON:	B.A. Rittersporn, Jr., Program Director
	(914) 428-7400
ADMINISTRATIVE UNIT:	A non-profit foundation devoted to study of questions affecting U.S. socioeconomic policies and problems.
BUDGET FY 1979–80:	*Not provided*
STAFFING:	*PROFESSIONAL STAFF*
	Social Work:
	Other Social Science:
	STUDENTS IN TRAINING
	Social Work:
	Other Social Science:

RESEARCH PURPOSES/
  ACTIVITIES: The Institute engages in periodic studies of all issues related to income security, including food stamps, benefits in the health service field and the like.

RESEARCH PRIORITIES:	*Profession Focussed;*	5, 8, 9, 10
	Fields of Investigation:	11, 12, 13, 14, 15, 16, 19, 20, 21, 23
	Special Populations:	24, 25, 26, 27
	Practice Modes:	35

PUBLICATIONS:	1. *The Journal* (Quarterly)
	2. *The Socioeconomic Newsletter* (Monthly)
	3. Publications list available on request.
DATE RESEARCH UNIT	
ESTABLISHED:	1974
DIRECTORY ENTRY DATE:	June, 1980

CODE NUMBER:	216011
CENTER NAME/ *ADDRESS:*	HUMAN SERVICES DESIGN LABORATORY School of Applied Social Sciences (1919) Case Western Reserve University Cleveland, Ohio 44106 (216) 368-2321
CONTACT PERSON:	Richard E. Isralowitz, Ph.D., Director (216) 368-2236
ADMINISTRATIVE UNIT:	Integral unit of the School of Applied Social Sciences, Case Western Reserve University, Cleveland.
BUDGET FY 1979–80:	$250,000

STAFFING:

PROFESSIONAL STAFF

Social Work:	2 Full time; 5 Part time
Other Social Science:	5 Full time; 4 part time

STUDENTS IN TRAINING

Social Work:	8 Ph.D.; 1 M.S.S.A.
Other Social Science:	

RESEARCH PURPOSES/
  ACTIVITIES:

To provide applied research and technical assistance to human service organizations confronted with issues of program evaluation; to provide a setting for SASS faculty to conduct research and technical assistance activities in their fields of expertise for human service agencies; to provide a training ground in applied research and new service technologies for graduate students of the SASS; to provide a means whereby pertinent academic and training curriculum materials, reflecting the needs and problems areas of human service providers, can be developed.

RESEARCH PRIORITIES:

Profession Focussed:	2, 6, 8, 9, 10
Fields of Practice:	11, 12, 13, 15, 17, 18, 19, 22, 23
Special Populations:	24, 25, 27
Practice Modes:	

PUBLICATIONS:	1. Publications list available on request.
DATE RESEARCH UNIT ESTABLISHED:	1969
DIRECTORY ENTRY DATE:	June, 1980

CODE NUMBER: 503011

CENTER NAME/
    ADDRESS: REGIONAL RESEARCH INSTITUTE FOR
                       HUMAN SERVICES
                       Portland State University (1964)
                       P.O. Box 751
                       Portland, Oregon 92707
                       (503) 229-4040

CONTACT PERSON: Arthur C. Emlen, Director
                       (503) 229-4040

ADMINISTRATIVE UNIT: Integral unit of Portland State University, Port-
                       land; and affiliated with School of Social
                       Work.

BUDGET FY: 1979–80: $1,128,000

STAFFING: PROFESSIONAL STAFF
                           Social Work: 7 Full time; 2 Part
                                                 time
                           Other Social Science: 15 Full time; 3 Part
                                                 time

                       STUDENTS IN TRAINING
                           Social Work: 18 Part time
                           Other Social Science: 3 Part time

RESEARCH PURPOSES/
    ACTIVITIES: To engage in a broad range of applied social
                       work and social science research which
                       improves the delivery of human services. The
                       Institute also sponsors a year-long specialized
                       concentration in Community Mental Health
                       Program Evaluation for second year MSW
                       students.

RESEARCH PRIORITIES: *Profession Focussed:*   2, 4, 6, 7, 8, 9
                       Fields of Practice: 15, 17, 19, 23
                       Special Populations: 27
                       Practice Modes: 30, 31, 32, 33, 34, 35,
                                                 36, 37, 38

PUBLICATIONS: 1. Publications list available on request.

DATE RESEARCH UNIT
ESTABLISHED: 1972

DIRECTORY ENTRY DATE: July, 1980

CODE NUMBER:	215011
CENTER NAME/	
ADDRESS:	CENTER FOR THE STUDY OF SOCIAL WORK PRACTICE
	School of Social Work (1919)
	University of Pennsylvania
	3701 Locust Walk/C3
	Philadelphia, Pennsylvania 19104
	(215) 243-5511
CONTACT PERSON:	Richard J. Estes, D.S.W., Director
	(215) 243-5531
ADMINISTRATIVE UNIT:	Integral unit of the School of Social Work, University of Pennsylvania, Philadelphia.
BUDGET FY 1979–80:	$160,000

STAFFING:

PROFESSIONAL STAFF

Social Work:	11 part time
Other Social Science:	6 Part time

STUDENTS IN TRAINING

Social Work:	6 D.S.W.' 2 M.S.W.
Other Social Science:	2 Ph.D.; 1 M.A.

RESEARCH PURPOSES/
  ACTIVITIES:

The Center engages in theory-guided, systematic, inquiry into the knowledge base of professional social work as practiced in a variety of forms across a broad range of institutional ᾽ settings. Assists with research education of masters and doctoral students and offers a post-doctoral research Fellowship Program to experienced scholars, researchers, and social work practitioners.

RESEARCH PRIORITIES:

Profession Focussed:	3, 9
Fields of Practice:	11, 15, 16, 17, 23, International Social Work, Racism
Special Populations:	24, 25, 26, 27, Aged
Practice Modes:	32, 35, 36, 38

PUBLICATIONS:	1. Publications list available on request, including *Reprint Series.*
DATE RESEARCH UNIT	
ESTABLISHED:	1976
DIRECTORY ENTRY DATE:	June, 1980

CODE NUMBER:	215021
CENTER NAME/ ADDRESS:	CENTER FOR SOCIAL POLICY AND COMMUNITY DEVELOPMENT Temple University School of Social Administration (1969) 1500 North Broad Street Philadelphia, Pennsylvania 19122 (215) 787-8621
CONTACT PERSON:	Dr. Seymour Rosenthal, Director (215) 787-7491
ADMINISTRATIVE UNIT:	Department of School of Social Administration, Temple University.
BUDGET FY 1979-80:	Not available.
STAFFING:	*PROFESSIONAL STAFF*

	Social Work:	12 Full time; 2 Part time
	Other Social Science:	10 Full time
	STUDENTS IN TRAINING	
	Social Work:	5
	Other Social Science:	0

RESEARCH PURPOSES/ ACTIVITIES:	For over ten years, CSPD has been involved in: (1) policy intervention into the planning and implementation of human service and housing systems (2) provision of continuing education for policy makers, practitioners within the human service and housing fields, and (3) operation of an educational learning center, primarily for students of the School of Social Administration.

RESEARCH PRIORITIES:	*Profession Focussed:*	2, 3, 5, 6
	Fields of Practice:	11, 15, 16, 17, 19, 20, 23
	Special Populations:	24, 25, 26, 28, Disabled
	Practice Modes:	32, 33, 34, 35, 36, 37, 38

PUBLICATIONS:	1. *Training Manual for Agencies Serving Older Adults*
	2. *Boarding Home Study of Philadelphia*
	3. *Interpersonal Skills Guide*
	4. *Continuing Education, A Collaborative Framework*
	5. *Public Housing and Residential Security*
	6. *Mental Health Planning Guide*

DATE RESEARCH UNIT
  ESTABLISHED: 1970

DIRECTORY ENTRY DATE: July, 1980

CODE NUMBER:	809011
CENTER NAME/	
ADDRESS:	SCIENTIFIC RESEARCH UNIT
	Graduate School of Social Work (1935)
	University of Puerto Rico
	Rio Piedras Campus
	Puerto Rico 00931
	(809) 764-0000 Ext. 2306, 2257
CONTACT PERSON:	Dr. Carmen F.Q. Rodriquez, Director
	(809) 764-0000 Ext. 2333 Or 2353
ADMINISTRATIVE UNIT:	Integral unit in Graduate School of Social Work, Rio Piedras Campus, Puerto Rico
BUDGET FY 1979–80:	Not available
STAFFING:	*PROFESSIONAL STAFF*

PROFESSIONAL STAFF
Social Work: 3 Part time
Other Social Science: 0

STUDENTS IN TRAINING
Social Work: 0
Other Social Science: 0

RESEARCH PURPOSES/
ACTIVITIES: To conduct research in the social welfare area with particular attention to the evaluation of social welfare programs. To carry out research related to curriculum issues, and social work education.

RESEARCH PRIORITIES:
Profession Focussed: 2, 3, 7, 8, 9
Fields of Practice: 12, 13, 15, 16, 17
Special Populations: 24
Practice Modes: 33, 38

PUBLICATIONS: 1. Publications list available on request.

DATE RESEARCH UNIT
ESTABLISHED: 1955

DIRECTORY ENTRY DATE: May, 1980

CODE NUMBER:	401013
CENTER NAME/ ADDRESS:	FOSTER PARENTS PLAN INTERNATIONAL (1937) 155 Plan Way Warwick, Rhode Island 02887 (401) 738-5600
CONTACT PERSON:	Anthony J. DiBella, Assistant Director of Field Services for Research (401) 738-5600
ADMINISTRATIVE UNIT:	FPPI is an internationally based organization providing for the needs of children in developing countries.
BUDGET FY 1979–80	Not provided

STAFFING:
PROFESSIONAL STAFF
Social Work: 1 Part time
Other Social Science: 1 Full time; 1 Part time

STUDENTS IN TRAINING
Social Work: 0
Other Social Science: 0

RESEARCH PURPOSES/ ACTIVITIES: To support the activities of the Foster Parents Plan International through research and knowledge-building.

RESEARCH PRIORITIES:
Profession Focussed: 8, 9
Fields of Practice: 14, 15, 16, 20, 21
Special Populations: 24
Practice Modes: 30, 31, 32

PUBLICATIONS: 1. *Annual Report* (Yearly)

DATE RESEARCH UNIT ESTABLISHED: 1979

DIRECTORY ENTRY DATE: April, 1980

CODE NUMBER: 615012

CENTER NAME/
  ADDRESS: JOHN F. KENNEDY CENTER FOR RESEARCH
                            ON EDUCATION AND HUMAN DEVELOP-
                            MENT (1965)
                            Box 40 Peabody College
                            Vanderbilt University
                            Nashville, Tennessee 37203
                            (615) 327-8242

CONTACT PERSON: Janet M. Rosemergy, Coordinator of Informa-
                            tion Services
                            (615) 327-8240

ADMINISTRATIVE UNIT: The Center is a University-sponsored, multi-
                            discipline unit serving the active Vanderbilt
                            University Community.

BUDGET FY 1979–80:   Not identified

STAFFING: *PROFESSIONAL STAFF*
                              Social Work: 0
                              Other Social Science: 46 Full time
                            STUDENTS IN TRAINING
                              Social Work: 0
                              Other Social Science: 10 Full time

RESEARCH PURPOSES/
  ACTIVITIES: One of twelve national centers for research
                            on mental retardation and related aspects of
                            human development. Conducts basic and
                            applied research on the psychological, educa-
                            tional, sociological, and ecological aspects of
                            mental retardation and other developmental
                            disorders, as well as on the broad area of
                            human development. Also serves as a labora-
                            tory for developing, evaluating, and dissemi-
                            nating innovative educational practices, espe-
                            cialy for developmentally delayed and other
                            exceptional children.

RESEARCH PRIORITIES: *Profession Focussed:*   3, 9
                            Fields of Practice: 13, 15, 17, 18, 19, 21
                            Special Populations: Families, Develop-
                                                     mentally Disabled
                            Practice Modes: 33, 34, 35

104

PUBLICATIONS:	1. *Research Progress Reports* (3 times yearly) 2. Extensive publications list available on request.
DATE RESEARCH UNIT *ESTABLISHED:*	1965
DIRECTORY ENTRY DATE:	June, 1980

CODE NUMBER:	512031
CENTER NAME/	
ADDRESS:	CENTER FOR SOCIAL WORK RESEARCH
	School of Social Work (1952)
	University of Texas at Austin
	Austin, Texas 78712
	(512) 471-4067
CONTACT PERSON:	David M. Austin, Ph.D., Administrator
	(512) 471-4067
ADMINISTRATIVE UNIT:	Integral unit of School of Social Work, University of Texas at Austin.
BUDGET FY 1976–77:	$1,000,000
STAFFING:	*PROFESSIONAL STAFF*

STAFFING: *PROFESSIONAL STAFF*

	Social Work:	8 Full time; 2 Part time
	Other Social Science:	10 Full time
	STUDENTS IN TRAINING	
	Social Work:	5 Ph.D.; 4 M.S.W.
	Other Social Science:	0

RESEARCH PURPOSES/
ACTIVITIES:

The Center is concerned with research, technical assistance, and training relevant to the concerns of human services. The Center operates a large continuing education program and maintains a computerized technical information service in the areas of child abuse and neglect.

RESEARCH PRIORITIES:

Profession Focussed:
Fields of Practice: 11, 15
Special Populations:
Practice Modes: 33, 38

PUBLICATIONS:

1. *Contact* (Quarterly)
2. Publications list available on request.

DATE RESEARCH UNIT
ESTABLISHED:

DIRECTORY ENTRY DATE: 1978

CODE NUMBER:	713011
CENTER NAME/ ADDRESS:	CENTER FOR SOCIAL SERVICES EVALUA-TION AND RESEARCH Graduate School of Social Work (1970) University of Houston Houston, Texas 77004 (713) 749-3814 Ext. 25
CONTACT PERSON:	Dr. Daniel Jennings, Dean (713) 749-3814 Ext. 25
ADMINISTRATIVE UNIT:	Integral unit of the Graduate School of Social Work, University of Houston.
BUDGET FY 1979–80:	Not available
STAFFING:	*PROFESSIONAL STAFF*

Social Work: 4 Full time
Other Social Science:

STUDENTS IN TRAINING
Social Work:
Other Social Science:

RESEARCH PURPOSES/ ACTIVITIES:

The Center serves as a focal point for University-based research and evaluation in social services, social work prctice and related training. Provides expertise for other departments of the University, other institutions, and community agencies concerned with social welfare research and evaluation. Designs and implements research and evaluation studies in social service delivery.

RESEARCH PRIORITIES:

Profession Focussed:	3
Fields of Practice	All
Special Populations:	All
Practice Modes:	All

PUBLICATIONS: 1. List available on request.

DATE RESEARCH UNIT ESTABLISHED: 1968

DIRECTORY ENTRY DATE: May, 1980

CODE NUMBER:	817021
CENTER NAME/	
ADDRESS:	RESEARCH CENTER
	Graduate School of Social Work (1970)
	University of Texas at Arlington
	Arlington, Texas 76019
	(817) 273-3407
CONTACT PERSON:	Michael Lobb, Ph.D., Director
	(817) 273-3407
ADMINISTRATIVE UNIT:	Integral unit of the School of Social Work, University of Texas, Arlington

BUDGET FY 1976–77:

STAFFING:

PROFESSIONAL STAFF
  Social Work: 1 Full time; 2 Part time
  Other Social Science:
STUDENTS IN TRAINING
  Social Work:
  Other Social Science:

RESEARCH PURPOSES/
ACTIVITIES: The Center engages in applied social work research in the fields of alcoholism, aging, behavior modification, and social work education.

RESEARCH PRIORITIES:
  Profession Focussed: 3
  Fields of Practice: 11, 12, 18, Population Density
  Special Populations:
  Practice Modes:

PUBLICATIONS: 1. Publications list available on request.

DATE RESEARCH UNIT
ESTABLISHED:

DIRECTORY ENTRY DATE: 1978

CODE NUMBER:	817033
CENTER NAME/	
ADDRESS:	ASSOCIATION FOR RETARDED CITIZENS 2709 Avenue E East Arlington, Texas 76011 (817) 261-4961
CONTACT PERSON:	Ronald Neman, Ph.D., Associate Director for Research (817) 261-4961
ADMINISTRATIVE UNIT:	
BUDGET FY 1979–80:	

STAFFING:	*PROFESSIONAL STAFF*
	  Social Work:
	  Other Social Science:
	STUDENTS IN TRAINING
	  Social Work:
	  Other Social Science:

RESEARCH PURPOSES/	
ACTIVITIES:	The Association engages in a broad range of research aimed at the prevention of mental retardation; environmental deprivation as a cause of mental retardation and research on alternative models of human service delivery.

RESEARCH PRIORITIES:	*Pofession Focussed:*	2, 3, 6, 7, 8, 9, 10
	Fields of Practice:	18
	Special Populations:	Retarded
	Practice Modes:	All

PUBLICATIONS:	1. Publications list available on request.
DATE RESEARCH UNIT	
ESTABLISHED:	
DIRECTORY ENTRY DATE:	April, 1980

CODE NUMBER:	206011
CENTER NAME/	
ADDRESS:	CENTER FOR SOCIAL WELFARE RESEARCH
	School of Social Work (1934)
	University of Washington
	Seattle, Washington 98105
	(206) 543-6888
CONTACT PERSON:	Michael J. Austin, Ph.D., Director
	(206) 543-6888
ADMINISTRATIVE UNIT:	Integral unit of the School of Social Work, University of Washington, Seattle
BUDGET FY 1979–80:	$350,000

STAFFING:

PROFESSIONAL STAFF

Social Work:	3 Full time; 7 Part time
Other Social Science:	3 Full time; 1 Part time

STUDENTS IN TRAINING

Social Work:	7 Part time
Other Social Science:	0

RESEARCH PURPOSES/
ACTIVITIES:

The Center works toward solving human services problems through the conduct of applied research and program development; and, participates in collaborative research with other schools in the University.

RESEARCH PRIORITIES:

Profession Focused:	3, Social Work Societies/ Organizations
Fields of Practice:	12, 14, 15, 16, 17
Special Populations:	25, 26, Aged
Practice Modes:	33

PUBLICATIONS:	1. Publications list available on request.
DATE RESEARCH UNIT	
ESTABLISHED:	1974
DIRECTORY ENTRY DATE:	July, 1980

CODE NUMBER:	304011
CENTER NAME/	
ADDRESS;	RESEARCH COMMITTEE
	West Virginia University (1942)
	School of Social Work
	708 Allen Hall
	Morgantown, West Virginia 26506
CONTACT PERSON:	Roger A. Lohmann, Ph.D., Coordinator
	Graduate Studies and Research
ADMINISTRATIVE UNIT:	Integral unit of West Virginia University
	School of Social Work.
BUDGET FY 1976-77:	Not available
STAFFING:	PROFESSIONAL STAFF

STAFFING:

PROFESSIONAL STAFF
Social Work: 5 Part time
Other Social Science: 0

STUDENTS IN TRAINING
Social Work:
Other Social Science:

RESEARCH PURPOSES/
   ACTIVITIES: The principal activity of the Committee has been the formation of an ad-hoc Committee on research which will: (1) define problems of mutual interest to School faculty; (2) survey social work faculty research interests; (3) survey faculty in other university schools and departments for their research interests; and, (4) negotiate with state departments for researchable problems.

RESEARCH PRIORITIES: Profession Focussed:
Fields of Practice: 11, 15, Sexuality, Financial Management

Special Populations:
Practice Modes: 35

PUBLICATIONS: 1. *Social Welfare in Appalachia* (Annual)

DATE RESEARCH UNIT
   ESTABLISHED:

DIRECTORY ENTRY DATE: 1978

CODE NUMBER:	414011
CENTER NAME/ ADDRESS:	CENTER FOR ADVANCED STUDIES IN HUMAN SERVICES

University of Wisconsin - Milwaukee (1963)
School of Social Welfare
P.O. Box 786
Milwaukee, Wisconsin 53201
(414) 963-6035

CONTACT PERSON: Lee H. Bowker, Director
(414) 963-6035

ADMINISTRATIVE UNIT: Integral unit of the School of Social Work, University of Wisconsin, Milawukee, Wisconsin.

BUDGET FY 1979–80: $50,000

STAFFING:

PROFESSIONAL STAFF
Social Work:	4 Full time
Other Social Science:	2 Full time; 3 Part time

STUDENTS IN TRAINING
Social Work:	0
Other Social Science:	0

RESEARCH PURPOSES/ ACTIVITIES:

To increase knowledge about individual and social behavior and their implications for designing human services; to assist local, state, and national constituencies improve the planning, implementation, management and delivery of needed programs and services; and to provide support for School of Social Welfare faculty and students to engage in research promoting the growth and application of human service knowledge and technology.

RESEARCH PRIORITIES:
Profession Focussed:	3, 7, 8, 9
Fields of Practice:	13, 15, 17, 23
Special Populations:	24, 25, 26, 27, Administrators
Practice Modes:	32, 34, 35, 36

PUBLICATIONS:	1. Publications list available on request.
DATE RESEARCH UNIT ESTABLISHED:	1975
DIRECTORY ENTRY DATE:	May, 1980

CODE NUMBER:	608021
CENTER NAME/	
ADDRESS:	CENTER FOR EVALUATION RESEARCH, TRAINING AND PROGRAM DEVELOPMENT
	University of Wisconsin - Madison (1922)
	School of Social Work
	425 Henry Mall
	Madison, Wisconsin 53706
	(608) 262-1407 or 262-5791
CONTACT PERSON:	Dr. Andre Delbecq, Director
	(608) 263-6336
ADMINISTRATIVE UNIT:	Integral Unit of the University of Wisconsin, School of Social Work, Madison, Wisconsin.
BUDGET FY 1976–77:	Not available

STAFFING:

PROFESSIONAL STAFF

Social Work:	2 Full time
Other Social Science:	2 Full time; 1 Part time

STUDENTS IN TRAINING

Social Work:	3 Part time
Other Social Science:	3 Part time

RESEARCH PURPOSES/
ACTIVITIES: The Center engages in research on evaluation processes and methodologies for human services, program development and administration as well as research training for human services.

RESEARCH PRIORITIES:
Profession Focussed:
Fields of Practice:
Special Populations:
Practice Modes: 33, 38

PUBLICATIONS: 1. Publications list available on request.

DATE RESEARCH UNIT
ESTABLISHED:

DIRECTORY ENTRY DATE: 1978

V CENTER RESEARCH PRIORITIES BY SUBSTANTIVE AREA AND CENTER CODE NUMBER

Social Work Profession Focussed

1. *History:* 202013, 202103, 202083, 413011
2. *Manpower:* 201011, 201022, 202013, 202043, 202063, 202083, 202093, 202121, 202131, 209011, 212063, 212073, 212113, 212123, 212151, 215021, 216011, 303012, 301023, 312053, 503011, 504011, 601011, 617011, 809011, 817033
3. *Education/Training:* 201022, 202013, 202033, 202043, 202063, 202073, 202083, 202093, 202121, 206011, 209011, 212011, 212053, 212063, 212073, 212083, 212093, 212113, 212123, 212151, 215011, 215021, 301023, 303012, 312021, 312053, 319011, 404011, 413011, 414011, 415011, 502011, 504011, 516011, 601011, 615012, 713011, 808011, 809011, 817021, 817033
4. *Ethics/Values:* 202013, 202083, 209011, 212123, 212151, 503011
5. *Interprofessional Relationships:* 202013, 202023, 202073, 202083, 209011, 212073, 212113, 212151, 215021, 301011, 312011, 312053, 312061, 415011, 516011, 601011, 617011, 914013
6. *Professional Community Relations:* 202013, 202023, 202043, 202073, 202083, 202093, 202103, 203011, 209011, 212053, 212093, 215021, 216011, 312011, 312053, 415011, 503011, 504021, 601011, 817033
7. *Standards/Practice:* 201011, 202013, 202023, 202043, 202083, 202093, 212053, 212083, 212103, 212113, 301023, 312021, 312053, 312061, 414011, 415011, 503011, 504011, 504021, 516011, 601011, 809011, 817033
8. *Service Utilization:* 201022, 202013, 202023, 202043, 202073, 202083, 202121, 209011, 212023, 212033, 212043, 212073, 212103, 212113, 212123, 212133, 212151, 216011, 301011, 301033, 312011, 312033, 312053, 319011, 401013, 414011, 415011, 503011, 504021, 516011, 601011, 617011, 808011, 809011, 817033, 914013
9. *Service Effectiveness:* 202013, 202023, 202043, 202056, 202063, 202073, 202083, 202103, 209011, 212023, 212033, 212043, 212063, 212073, 212103, 212123, 212133, 212151, 215011, 216011, 301011, 301033, 303012, 312011, 312021, 312033, 312053, 312061, 319011, 401013, 414011, 415011, 503011, 504021, 516011, 601011, 615012, 617011, 808011, 809011, 817033, 914013

10. *Benefit/Cost Analysis:* 202013, 202056, 202073, 202083, 202113, 212073, 212123, 216011, 301033, 312011, 312033, 312053, 312061, 319011, 617011, 817033, 914013

Fields of Practice

11. *Aging/Aged:* 201011, 202033, 202056, 202093, 202121, 202131, 212011, 212053, 212083, 212093, 212113, 212151, 215011, 215021, 216011, 218011, 301011, 301023, 303012, 304011, 413011, 512031, 516011, 601011, 617011, 617041, 713011, 817021, 914013

12. *Alcoholism/Drug Addiction:* 201011, 202056, 202083, 202093, 202121, 212093, 212113, 206011, 216011, 212151, 218011, 301011, 301023, 312011, 415011, 516011, 713011, 808011, 809011, 817021, 914013

13. *Crime/Delinquency:* 201011, 202083, 202121, 212053, 212093, 212113, 202151, 216011, 218011, 301011, 301023, 312011, 312061, 319011, 414011, 415011, 516011, 615012, 713011, 808011, 809011, 914013

14. *Economic Security:* 202033, 202043, 202083, 202131, 206011, 212011, 212043, 212093, 212113, 212151, 301011, 312061, 401013, 415011, 516011, 601011, 617031, 617041, 713011, 914013

15. *Family/Child Welfare:* 201011, 202043, 202063, 202083, 202093, 202121, 202131, 206011, 209011, 212011, 212023, 212033, 212053, 212063, 212073, 212093, 212103, 212113, 212123, 212151, 215011, 215021, 216011, 218011, 301011, 301033, 303012, 304011, 312011, 312021, 312061, 319011, 401013, 404011, 413011, 414011, 415011, 503011, 504011, 512031, 516011, 601011, 615012, 713011, 809011, 914013

16. *Health/Medical Care:* 201011, 202043, 202056, 202083, 202093, 202131, 203011, 206011, 209011, 212093, 212103, 212113, 212151, 215011, 215021, 301011, 303012, 312011, 312053, 312061, 401013, 404011, 415011, 504011, 516011, 601011, 617011, 617021, 617031, 617051, 713011, 809011, 914013

17. *Mental Health:* 201011, 202056, 202083, 202093, 202121, 206011, 209011, 212063, 212093, 212103, 212113, 212151, 215011, 215021, 216011, 218011, 301011, 301033, 312011, 312053, 312061, 319011, 413011, 414011, 415011, 503011, 504011, 516011, 601011, 615012, 617011, 617021, 617051, 713011, 809011

18. *Mental Retardation:* 202023, 202083, 202093, 202131, 212093, 212103, 212113, 216011, 303012, 312061, 415011, 504011, 516011, 615012, 617011, 617021, 713011, 817021, 817033

19. *Physically Handicapped:* 202043, 202063, 202083, 202093, 202131, 212093, 212103, 212113, 212133, 212151, 215021, 216011, 303012, 312043, 312061, 415011, 503011, 516011, 615012, 617011, 617021, 713011, 808011, 914013

20. *Housing/Urban Development:* 202013, 202033, 202073, 202083, 202103, 202113, 202121, 202131, 212043, 212053, 212093, 212103, 212113, 212151, 215021, 401013, 415011, 516011, 601011, 617011, 713011, 914013

21. *Early Childhood Education:* 202083, 202121, 209011, 212063, 212093, 212113, 212123, 312061, 401013, 415011, 516011, 615012, 713011, 914013

22. *Civil Rights/Civil Liberties:* 202033, 202043, 202083, 202103, 202121, 202131, 212043, 212053, 212093, 212113, 216011, 415011, 516011, 601011, 713011

23. *Employment/Unemployment:* 202033, 202083, 202121, 202131, 212011, 212043, 212053, 212063, 212093, 212113, 212151, 215011, 215023, 312061, 414011, 415011, 503011, 516011, 601011, 617031, 617041, 713011, 808011, 914013

   23A. *Other Fields of Practice*
   a. *Energy:* 202073
   b. *Family LIfe Education:* 212073
   c. *Homemaker Services:* 212083
   d. *Industrial Social Work:* 209011
   e. *International Social Work:* 201022, 212151, 215011
   f. *Jewish Communal Service:* 212033
   g. *Population:* 817021
   h. *Public Health:* 202093
   i. *Rural Social Work:* 516011
   j. *School Social Work:* 203011
   k. *Sexuality:* 304011
   l. *Transportation:* 202043
   m. *White Racism:* 215011

Special Populations

24. *Poor:* 201011, 202013, 202033, 202043, 202056, 202083, 202093, 202103, 202131, 209011, 212011, 212033, 212053, 212063, 212073, 212093, 212103, 212113, 212123, 212151, 215011,

215023, 216011, 303012, 312011, 312053, 312061, 319011, 401013, 414011, 415011, 504011, 516011, 601011, 617031, 713011, 808011, 809011, 914013

25. *Minorities*: 201011, 202033, 202043, 202056, 202083, 202093, 202103, 202131, 206011, 209011, 212011, 212033, 212043, 212053, 212063, 212073, 212093, 212103, 212113, 212123, 212151, 215011, 216011, 215021, 218011, 303012, 312011, 312053, 312061, 319011, 404011, 413011, 414011, 415011, 504011, 516011, 601011, 617031, 713011, 808011, 914013

26. *Women*: 201011, 202033, 202063, 202083, 202093, 202103, 206011, 212011, 212033, 212053, 212093, 212103, 212113, 212123, 212151, 215011, 215021, 312011, 312053, 312061, 319011, 404011, 413011, 414011, 415011, 504011, 516011, 601011, 617031, 713011, 914013

27. *Youth*: 201011, 202033, 202083, 202093, 202103, 202131, 212011, 212033, 212053, 212063, 212073, 212093, 212103, 212113, 212151, 215011, 216011, 218011, 301011, 312011, 312021, 312053, 312061, 319011, 404011, 414011, 415011, 503011, 504011, 516011, 601011, 617031, 713011, 914013

28. *Other Special Populations*
    a. *Chronically Ill*: 212083, 617021
    b. *Developmentally Disabled*: 202023, 215021, 615012, 617021, 617051, 817033
    c. *Girls*: 212123
    d. *Indochinese Refugees*: 202043
    e. *Moderate Income*: 202113
    f. *Native Americans*: 218011, 303012
    g. *Paraprofessionals*: 212063
    h. *Single Parents*: 301033
    i. *Veterans*: 202056
    j. *Visually Impaired*: 212133
    k. *Industrial Workers*: 212151

Practice Modes

30. *Social Casework*: 201011, 202083, 212011, 212053, 212073, 212103, 212113, 212151, 312021, 401013, 413011, 415011, 503011, 504011, 504021, 516011, 601011, 713011, 808011, 817033

31. *Social Group Work*: 201011, 202083, 212011, 212023, 212033, 212053, 212103, 212113, 212133, 212151, 312021, 401013, 415011, 503011, 504011, 504021, 516011, 601011, 713011, 817033

32. *Community Organization*: 202033, 202083, 202093, 209011, 212011, 212023, 212033, 212043, 212093, 212113, 212151, 215011, 215021, 218011, 319011, 401013, 414011, 415011, 503011, 516011, 601011, 713011, 817033

33. *Social Administration*: 201011, 202073, 202083, 206011, 209011, 212011, 212043, 212113, 212151, 215023, 218011, 301023, 301033, 312011, 312053, 312061, 319011, 415011, 503011, 504021, 512031, 516011, 601011, 608021, 615012, 713011, 809011, 817033

34. *Social Planning*: 202013, 202033, 202073, 202083, 202093, 212011, 212043, 212073, 212093, 212113, 212151, 215021, 218011, 301023, 303012, 312011, 312053, 312061, 319011, 404011, 414011, 415011, 503011, 504021, 601011, 615012, 713011, 817033

35. *Social Policy Analysis*: 201011, 202013, 202033, 202073, 202083, 202093, 202113, 202131, 212011, 212043, 212073, 212113, 212133, 212151, 215011, 215021, 218011, 301023, 303012, 304011, 312011, 312033, 312053, 312061, 319011, 404011, 414011, 415011, 503011, 601011, 612012, 617021, 617031, 617041, 617051, 713011, 817033, 914013

36. *Social Work Research*: 202083, 209011, 212011, 212073, 212113, 212151, 215011, 215021, 218011, 303012, 312053, 312061, 319011, 413011, 414011, 415011, 503011, 504021, 601011, 713011, 817033

37. *Consultation*: 202083, 202093, 212011, 212043, 212093, 212113, 212151, 215021, 218011, 301023, 303012, 312011, 312053, 319011, 415011, 503011, 504021, 713011, 817033

38. *Social Work Education*: 202083, 212073, 212093, 212113, 212151, 215011, 215021, 312053, 319011, 404011, 415011, 502011, 503011, 504011, 504021, 512031, 516011, 608021, 713011, 809011, 817033

APPENDIX
SOCIAL WELFARE RESEARCH CENTER
SURVEY QUESTIONNAIRE

Part I   Descriptive Information

1. Organization Name:_____
   Address_____

   _____

   _____

2. Executive Director Name_____
   Title_____
   Telephone Number (   )_____Extension_____
3. Director of Research_____
   Title_____
   Telephone Number_____
4. Name of Person Completing Questionnaire_____
   Title_____
   Telephone Number (   )_____Extension_____
5. Date organization established_____
6. Briefly describe the major purposes and activities of your organization (Do not exceed 100 words).
7. Does your organization have a system of local chapters or divisions?
   _____Yes   _____No
   If yes, please describe:

Part II.   Research Capabilities of Organization

(*NOTE:* For purposes of this questionnaire, "research" includes all organizational activities relating to the systematic gathering, organization, analysis and dissemination of data including the gathering of periodic service statistics, program evaluation, and more specialized research studies.)

8. Does your organization have a formally organized research department or research unit? _____YES   _____NO
   8a. If yes to question 8, briefly describe the *major purposes* of your organization's research unit. (Please limit response to 50 words).
   8b. If yes to question 8, please describe the *major activities* of your organization's research unit. (Please limit response to 50 words).
   8c. If yes to question 8, how many years has your organization's research unit been in existence?
   _____years.
   8d. If yes to question 8, how many persons work *directly* under the auspices of the research unit?
   Number of persons working full time_____
   Number of persons working part time_____

9. Approximately how many staff members work on organization-related research but *are not members of a formally organized research unit* or department?

        Number of persons working full time_____

        Number of persons working part time_____

10. Please indicate on the following chart the total numbers of persons *working full or part time on organization-related research* of any type by educational background and professional discipline.

	PERSONS WITH FORMAL SOCIAL WORK TRAINING (i.e. holders of BSW, MSW, or DSW degrees)		PERSONS WITH DEGREES IN OTHER SOCIAL SCIENCES DISCIPLINES (e.g. Sociology, Psychology, etc.)	
	Full Time	Part Time	Full Time	Part Time
Professional Staff				
Baccalaureate	_____	_____	_____	_____
Masters	_____	_____	_____	_____
Doctoral	_____	_____	_____	_____
Other (specify)	_____	_____	_____	_____
Students in Training				
Baccalaureate	_____	_____	_____	_____
Masters	_____	_____	_____	_____
Doctoral	_____	_____	_____	_____
Other (specify)	_____	_____	_____	_____

11. Does your organization purchase research services from research departments or units located in other organizations? _____YES _____NO

    11a. If yes to question 11, from which type of organization(s) does your organization purchase research services?

    _____Universities _____non-profit research institutes _____other (specify)_

    11b. If yes to question 11, approximately what percent of your organization's total research effort is purchased from research contractors?

    _____ %

    11c. On the whole, to what extent has your organization been satisfied with the quality of research purchased under contract with outside organizations?

               _____very satisfied

               _____satisfied

               _____dissatisfied

               _____very dissatisfied

    Please explain:

Part III.   Research Priorities

13. Research units tend to specialize by areas of expertise, fields of practice, methodological preferences, and/or problem areas. Please indicate below the *relative priority* which characterizes your unit's research interests. Also of interest are the numbers and types of studies your unit is currently involved in or has recently completed.

For the *ranking* of research priorities, please use the following scale:

0 = not a research priority
1 = low priority
2 = moderate priority
3 = high priority

	Priority Ranking (0–3)	No. of Studies in Progress	No. of Studies Completed in last 2 years
13A. ORGANIZATION FOCUSSED RESEARCH EFFORTS			
History			
Manpower			
Education/Training			
Ethics/Values			
Interprofessional Relationships			
Professional Community Relation			
Standard/Practices			
Service Utilization			
Service Effectiveness			
Benefit/Cost Analysis			
13B. *Research by Fields of Practice*			
Aging/Aged			
Alcoholism/Drug Addiction			
Crime/Delinquency			
Economic Security			
Family/Child Welfare			
Health/Medical Care			
Mental Health			
Mental Retardation			
Physically handicapped			
Housing/Urban Development			
Early/Childhood Education			
Civil Rights/Civil Liberties			

Employment/
  Unemployment   _____   _____   _____
Other   _____   _____   _____

13C. *Research on Special*
  Populations
  Poor   _____   _____   _____
  Minorities   _____   _____   _____
  Women   _____   _____   _____
  Youth   _____   _____   _____
  Other_____   _____   _____   _____
  Other_____   _____   _____   _____
13D. *Research on Social*
  Intervention Methods
  Social Casework   _____   _____   _____
  Social Group Work   _____   _____   _____
  Community Organ-
    ization   _____   _____   _____
  Social Administration   _____   _____   _____
  Social Planning   _____   _____   _____
  Social Policy Analysis   _____   _____   _____
  Social Work Research   _____   _____   _____
  Consultation   _____   _____   _____
  Social Work Education   _____   _____   _____
  Other_____   _____   _____   _____
  Other_____   _____   _____   _____

Part IV.   *Sources of Agency/Organization Research Support*

14. Including all costs for salaries, benefits, materials, supplies, etc., what do you estimate to have been your agency's total expenditures for research related activities during fiscal year 1979?
  $_____ .
15. Please show the approximate percentage (%) of research support to your organization from each of the following research support sources.

	Basic Subsidies	Grants	Contracts	TOTAL
A. *Organization's Own Resources*	____	____	____	____
B. *Private Sources*				
Foundations	____	____	____	____
Individuals	____	____	____	____
Other	____	____	____	____
C. *Public Sources*				
Local	____	____	____	____
State	____	____	____	____
Federal	____	____	____	____
Other	____	____	____	____

127

Part V.   Dissemination of Research Findings

16. During the past 24 months, approximate the number of reports of agency research that have been disseminated in the following ways:
17. Summary of findings reported at annual meetings of agency staff, board directors, etc. _____
18. Private reports to Funding or Accountability Sources _____
19. Summary of findings reported at National Meetings of relevant professional groups _____
20. Publications in national journals _____
21. Publication as chapters in books, monographs, etc. _____
22. Other forms of dissemination, please specify:
_____
_____

Part VI.   Unit Reports and Publications

23. The Center for the Study of Social Work Practice is interested in receiving additional information from your research unit, i.e., annual reports, list of publications, available article reprints, etc.
24. Please include here any other information which you feel would better help us understand the nature and type of research undertaken by your research department/unit.
25. Please list the name, frequency and price of any publications regularly issued by your organizations.

Name	Frequency	Price

YOUR COOPERATION WITH THIS SURVEY IS DEEPLY APPRECIATED.

About the Author

Richard J. Estes is Associate Professor of Social Work and Director of the Center for the Study of Social Work Practice at the University of Pennsylvania. He holds graduate degrees from the University of Pennsylvania and the University of California at Berkeley. Dr. Estes' research interests include international and comparative social welfare, employment and unemployment, mental health epidemiology, and small group dynamics. Dr. Estes has travelled extensively and, during 1978–1979, was a Senior Fulbright Lecturer to both the Institute for Advanced Social Work Education in Trondheim, Norway and the Teheran School of Social Work, Teheran, Iran. He lectures and consults widely and has authored numerous papers and research monographs on a variety of social work/social welfare topics.

Dr. Estes presently is completing work on three additional books: SOCIAL WORKERS IN HEALTH CARE (Warren H. Green, Inc., 1981); SOCIAL WORK PRACTICE: A PICTORIAL ESSAY (National Association of Social Workers, 1981); and, WORLD SOCIAL VULNERABILITY: THE SOCIAL PROGRESS OF NATIONS, 1968–1978 (in preparation).